Welles

Welles

Ben Walters

HAUS PUBLISHING • LONDON

4.2.05

To Eric,
Thanks for the
guidance shared
to a busy little
bitch boy.

Love Ben

First published in Great Britain in 2004 by
Haus Publishing Limited
26 Cadogan Court, Draycott Avenue
London SW3 3BX

A CIP catalogue record for this book is available from the British Library

ISBN 1-904341-80-2

Designed and typeset in Garamond by Falcon Oast Graphic Art
Printed and bound by Graphicom in Vicenza, Italy

Front cover: courtesy AKG Images
Back cover: courtesy Berlin Film Archive

For my parents, with love and thanks.

Contents

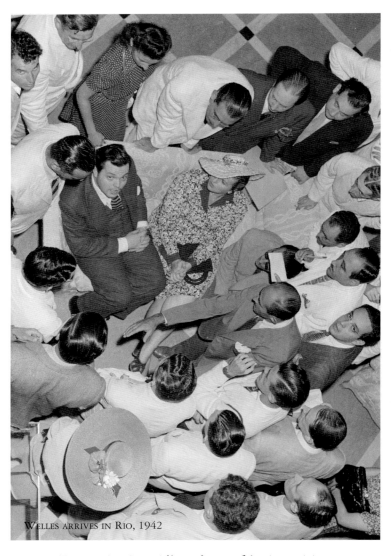

WELLES ARRIVES IN RIO, 1942

'Reputation is an idle and most false imposition;
oft got without merit, and lost without deserving.'

Iago in *Othello*, Act 2 Scene 3

Birth to Todd 1915–31

At 6am on 6 May 1915, the factory bells of Kenosha, Wisconsin, provided the first of George Orson Welles's many fanfares. The newborn was large, with a hint of the exotic about his almost Oriental eyes and rosebud mouth. Later he would say he had been conceived in Rio though, like many of his recollections, this probably illustrates his own powers of conception better than the actual biological event.

Born in 1872, Orson's father Richard Welles – 'Dick' – had by his mid-20s become a partner in a family firm creating patents for bicycle and automobile accessories. He had also developed a taste for the vaudeville and brothels of Chicago, barely two hours' train ride away from Kenosha. In 1903 Dick met 21-year-old Beatrice Ives, whose industrialist father had been all but ruined by the coal slump of the 1890s. A formidable, handsome woman, her charm and intellect were matched by aesthetic and musical ability and a 'rich and overpowering' voice.[1] The couple married that November and soon had a son, also called Richard, whose withdrawn nature endeared him to neither parent. Dick and Beatrice's marriage did not prove harmonious: he liked the horses and music halls; she gave choral recitals and campaigned for immigrants' rights and women's suffrage. By 1912 she was Kenosha's first female elected official while his career had stalled and his drinking increased. By the time their second son Orson was born a decade later, young Richard had also developed a severe stammer and social and behavioural problems.

Orson's debut brought a welcome and responsive focus to this fractured household, though it would arguably prove the catalyst for its collapse as well. Barely a year after the bright, loud, lusty child arrived, his introverted brother was packed off to the Todd School, a private school in Woodstock, Illinois, run along quasi-military lines by the forbidding Noble Hill. Beatrice, meanwhile, was spoon-feeding Shakespeare and the romantics to her beloved Orson. *The word 'genius'*, Welles reported, *was whispered into my ear the first thing I ever heard while I was still mewling in my crib, so it never occurred to me that I wasn't until middle age!*[2]

Beatrice was not alone in fostering such immoderate conviction in her son. Dr Maurice Bernstein, a 29-year-old physician summoned one day on house call unrelated to Orson, quickly became a still more ardent promoter of the precocious boy. A debonair, cultured, attractive Russian émigré, Bernstein became a regular caller on both the boy, to whom he gave a magic kit and puppet theatre, and his mother. He nicknamed Orson 'Pookles' and was called 'Dadda' in return. In 1918, the family – plus Bernstein – decamped to Chicago, funded by the sale of Dick's patents for $100,000. (He never worked again.)

Capital of the Midwest and the rival of New York in most respects, the city offered greater opportunities for Dick and Beatrice to indulge their mutually exclusive interests: his after-hours lifestyle saw his drinking increase to near-alcoholic levels while she established herself in musical society. Beatrice's melodious recitals were much praised – as was the precocious conversation of her apparently well-informed son. Orson's health, like Beatrice's, was not good (he had hay fever and asthma and later developed flat feet and back problems) and her home teaching seems to have taken up the considerable motivational resources she had previously devoted to social campaigning. Her attention was both indulgent and demanding: *children could be treated as adults as long as they were amusing. The moment you were boring, it*

Welles with one of his early devotees

was off to the nursery.[3] This fostered in Orson a *determination to escape the conditions of childhood*[4] extending to his applying wrinkles using a junior make-up kit – the beginning of a lifelong theatrical preoccupation with ageing.

Beatrice and Dick separated in 1919, though they remained on cordial terms, taking regular holidays *en famille* (again including Bernstein) at Grand Detour, a small, picturesque town outside Chicago. Orson's superior attitude, violent tantrums and pronounced sweet tooth earned him the nickname 'Georgie Porgie Pudding and Pie', but he also found rapt audiences for his puppet shows, ghost stories and Shakespearean digests.

In 1922 Beatrice contracted hepatitis and grew painfully weaker over the following two years. Her decline came as a profound shock to her doting son. Years later, Welles described the scene that greeted him when he visited Beatrice's sickbed on his ninth birthday. It was a dark, eerie tableau that resonated with many of the concerns Welles would explore throughout his life: storytelling, magic, darkness and the power of the spoken word. His mother *was a voice in the shadows, speaking Shakespeare*, the candles on his birthday cake the *fairy ring [of] a Sorceress*. Beatrice's death a few days later removed the towering presence of Orson's life to date, the parent whose demands and approval had been the bedrock of his imaginative activities. It was in effect the end of his childhood; from now on, it seems, he behaved on his own terms.

Having competed for Beatrice's attention throughout her illness, Dadda and Dick now switched their focus to Orson. (Young Richard, by now expelled from Todd, was barely acknowledged.) Dick and Dadda moved in together, even taking a trip to Europe that summer while Orson stayed with relatives. On their return the nine-year-old was sent to Madison, Wisconsin for psychological tests (he challenged the terms of the questions) and a brief spell at state school, where he mounted a public attack on the arts curriculum. For this he was photographed by the local paper, in anticipation of which he instructed Dadda to dispatch a suitably arty cravat. He also edited a summer camp magazine and on 19 February 1926 *The Madison Journal* (where Bernstein had contacts) published a tribute under the headline 'CARTOONIST, ACTOR, POET AND ONLY TEN'.

Dick and Dadda decided a state education was insufficient for their prodigy's needs and so, after having applied unsuccessfully to military school, Orson enrolled at Todd – which, thanks to his brother, he knew about *as criminals know about San Quentin.*[5] What he found that autumn was unexpected: control of Todd's 14 well-equipped acres was gradually passing from the intimidating Noble Hill to his son Roger, a charismatic, rangy 31-year-old known as 'Skipper', whom the boys treated more like an older brother than an authority figure. This energetic newcomer to education encouraged the pursuit of individual interests outside of the traditional curriculum. To Skipper Hill, learning was an adventure. *He was always younger than I was,*[6] Welles claimed – though this was another way of saying how old he seemed himself.

His arrival, after the start of term, was the source of some excitement: 'students stuck their head round the corner to see what kind of celebrity had arrived.'[7] Still only 11, Orson already had a disconcertingly adult bearing. He cultivated an air of exotic maturity, burning incense, wearing make-up, embellishing family yarns his father had spun him and dropping names like Houdini, Plato and Shakespeare. Unconcerned with close friendship, he became a campus character with a large, attentive audience – and the much-envied patronage of Skipper Hill. He pursued Skipper with disquieting directness. Already dabbling at doctors and nurses and (he claimed) used to fending off the advances of older men before his arrival at Todd, Welles recalled in frankly sexual terms his seduction of *this marvellous man with whom I was in love.*[8] To the alarm of Skipper's wife Hortense, Orson lounged coquettishly on the marital bed; much later he told Hill he was *the boy you could have had*,[9] but Hill's interest in the boy was purely pedagogic.

While at Todd Orson grew from a disconcerting child into a striking young man: at 13 he was six feet tall, no longer plump but languorous, with a feline habit of brushing his long dark hair from his high forehead, revealing his quick almond eyes. Throughout Welles's young life he entered into a profitable series of mentor relationships with older men, often homosexual, who looked on him with unusually intense affection. Whether or not there were ever physical exchanges, he was plainly aware of his sexual appeal. It is harder to say whether this boy – who seemed to his contemporaries 'void of any human relationship of needing and being needed'[10] – was also seeking the authority and support his uncultured father, now an alcoholic, couldn't provide. Orson was mortified by Dick's sporadic, sometimes drunken visits to Todd while Dick was baffled and alienated by his son's obsession with theatre.

Orson's allure lay in his blend of unnerving self-assurance and disarming deference, along with an invaluable legacy from his mother: a gorgeous, seductive purr of a voice that invited credulity and wonder. His voice broke early and to Woodstock's residents it must have seemed to be using Orson's pudgy frame as a mere vessel. Welles 'would always order his sodas in that big, booming voice of his, intimidating the hell out of the people around him.'[11] Once, sports coach Roskey recalled, 'I got him to open his mouth real wide and said, 'I want to take a picture of that mouth because some day it's going to be famous."[12] Orson opened wide and advanced on the camera, as if to gobble the transfixed thing up. It would not be the last extreme close-up of that mouth, nor the last time the camera would strain to see that voice.

Skipper soon became as dedicated to Orson's success as Dadda Bernstein had been. While hardly the restraining influence Dick and Dadda envisaged – 'I knew he was going to be a great man, and I tried to structure a life for him at Todd that wouldn't impede his brilliance at all'[13] – Hill was to prove perhaps the single most reliable, sustaining source of emotional support throughout Welles's life. For the time being this provided something like a family (Orson became a fixture at the Hills' home) and a license to avoid curricular pursuits. He attended class only to challenge the teachers, ignored sports and giggled through church. It was generally acknowledged that 'he had a beautiful voice, a lot of talent, but he was not easy as a person.'[14]

All Orson's energies went into the school's 200-seat theatre: weekly productions became the norm, from drag revues (a common feature of amateur and popular theatre of the time) overseen by Skipper to productions of the classics open to the general public. During his years at Todd Orson played Mary, Judas, Christ, a musical lead, an atomic scientist and dozens more. Already a veteran Chicago playgoer, Welles's consumption of theatre journals gave him a better grasp of the European avant-garde than many professional directors; he trained himself in set design, lighting, sound, music and make-up, and demonstrated astonishing confidence – even ruthlessness – as a script editor. As a director he was preternaturally assured, mounting Molière, Marlowe and *Everyman*. His *Julius Caesar* was, we are told, disqualified from a Chicago Drama League competition because of the two adult actors playing Antony and Cassius. Orson, then 15 years old, had played both roles. Meanwhile, he was also editing the school magazine and, thanks to Dadda's contacts, writing sophisticated if snide dramatic criticism for the *Highland Park News: last week I insinuated that there had been no real performance of opera in Ravinia and I think I was right.*[15]

While Orson's public life on stage and in print was making satisfying progress, his family life was troubled and upsetting. In 1927 Dick and Dadda had Orson's brother Richard committed to a mental institution, where he would spend the next decade. He was also all but removed from his father's will. The following year the hotel Dick had bought and lovingly tended at Grand Detour accidentally burned to the ground, precipitating the final stage of his alcohol-fuelled decline.

Young Orson had already travelled widely, visiting Europe, Cuba and other destinations with Dick, Dadda and the school. In the summer of 1930, he trailed to his *Highland Park News* readers a tour of China and Japan with his father: *All the clout, glamour, romance of the Orient will troop in Literary Caravan across the glowing lines of this: your favourite feature of your favourite journal*,[16] he promised. He did indeed deliver some impressive prose but most of the journey was spent nursing his inebriate father, who *felt he'd lost me in the great struggle for my psyche, not in my love for him, but in what I was going to be . . . I knew he'd come to the end of the road.*[17] On their return, Orson followed the Hills' advice that he should refuse to see Dick until he was sober. Dick – unable, of course, to meet such a demand – died that Christmas, aged 58, alone in a Chicago hotel room. Beatrice's death had deprived Orson of his most cherished admirer and forced the boy into emotional self-sufficiency; now the adolescent felt that in remaining distant from his weak father he had somehow caused his death. Welles later claimed never to have forgiven himself for deserting Dick.

Following a traumatic funeral, at which Orson apparently clashed with his fearsome estranged grandmother, he was told to select his own guardian. Skipper refused the nomination and it fell to Dadda Bernstein to administer Orson's inheritance of $37,000, to be made over to him at the age of 25. Back at Todd Orson applied himself to his main project, an ambitious, abortive attempt to amalgamate a number of Shakespeare's history plays; there was also the formality of academic graduation. Thanks to last-minute coaching from a more conscientious classmate, Orson finished top of the class.

While Dadda and Skipper mulled over which Ivy League school he should apply to, Orson took out notices in *Billboard* magazine advertising his services playing 'Stock Characters, Heavies, Juveniles' and offering to contribute his own funds towards productions, presumably on condition of his being cast. Bitterly opposed to a theatrical career, Dadda suggested a walking and painting tour in Ireland and Scotland as distraction. Four days later, on 31 August 1931, the 16-year-old orphan set off alone to cross the ocean. Was the world ready for him?

Galway to Broadway 1931–34

'He became a legend almost at once . . . Everyone started talking about him . . . that he had walked round the Great Wall of China; that he had played in Greek plays in Greece and had Turkish baths in Turkey.'[18]

Lady Longford, sponsor of the Gate Theatre, Dublin

When he landed at Galway, Welles was without an audience of indulgent elders for the first time. Nevertheless, he showed characteristic self-assurance in his unplanned travels: touring the west coast of Ireland by donkey-drawn cart, he kept Dadda and Skipper updated through eloquent, colourful letters unashamedly *DEALING SOLELY WITH MYSELF.*[19] He was confident that *my week with the band of gypsies, my mountain-climbs, my night in a quagmire, and finally, the auctioning of [my donkey] at the Clifden fair – should all make tolerably interesting after-dinner tales.*[20]

Orson's carefree jaunt lasted until his arrival in Dublin in autumn 1931, where he was disappointed to find its citizens less susceptible to his charismatic patter than country landlords or island farmers. Within 48 hours, however, he had presented his (largely fabricated) credentials at the Gate Theatre, Ireland's most ambitious and accomplished avant-garde company. Only three years old, it was already succeeding in broadening the concerns of the Irish stage, particularly in its openness to European influences. Its proprietors – the dashing, foppish, outrageous Micheál Mac Liammóir and his more proper but equally zealous English lover, Hilton Edwards –

were devoted to each other and their fledgling theatre, overseeing its every aspect. Their anti-naturalistic 'Theatre Theatrical' would profoundly influence Welles's work, and indeed life.

Edwards and Mac Liammóir happened to be looking for a factotum who could both paint scenery and handle publicity – fields in which Welles was already adept. They were also casting for their upcoming production, *Jew Süss*. One of the leads – the boorish, scheming Duke – was just the type of larger-than-life villain Orson had developed a taste for at Todd, allowing for expansive acting and grotesque make-up. Even Orson acknowledged his audition to be pure *J. Worthington Ham*[22] yet Mac Liammóir saw 'all the qualities of fine acting tearing their way through a chaos of inexperience'[23] and the boy was granted *the opportunity I have been praying for*.[24] Despite recognising the shortcomings of his technique, Orson showed little interest in improving it – he saw little need

'We found . . . a very tall young man with a chubby face, full, powerful lips, and disconcerting Chinese eyes . . . The voice, with its brazen transatlantic sonority, was already that of a preacher, a leader, a man of power; it bloomed and boomed its way through the dusty air of the scene dock as though it would crush the little Georgian walls and rip up the floor; he . . . surveyed us with magnificent patience as though here was our chance to do something beautiful at last – yes, sir – and were we going to take it?'

MAC LIAMMÓIR (PICTURED LEFT, WITH EDWARDS, SOME YEARS LATER) DESCRIBES WELLES'S ARRIVAL AT THE GATE THEATRE[21]

to investigate a character's psychology given that his barnstorming style was sufficient to wow an audience in itself.

Come the first night, 13 October 1931, Orson took to the stage *in the bliss of ignorance, like a baby on a trapeze.* All went well – too well. Inebriated by audience approval, his acting grew reckless and greedy. When his character referred to 'a bride fit for Solomon – he had a thousand wives, did he not?' a cry came from the stalls: 'That's a dirty black Protestant lie!' Disoriented by this unexpectedly potent voice in the darkness, Orson began to fluff lines and botch business. Finally he hurled himself down the stairs on the set in shamed desperation – and brought the house down with him. He gorged on the adulation.

The critics – including one from the *New York Times* – competed to praise the new discovery and, aided by his own efforts from the Gate press office and a newspaper column he wrote pseudonymously, 'young Welles' was soon a society attraction. Mac Liammóir observed that, though Orson was charming in private, 'when a stupid audience surrounded him . . . he would use them mercilessly, without shame or repulsion . . . trumpeting his jungle-laughter as one tinsel fable followed another.'[25] Mac Liammóir cast his boy wonder in half a dozen more roles over the next few months, mostly middle-aged heavies that tested Orson's make-up box more than his acting. Despite playing Fortinbras and the Ghost in Mac Liammóir's acclaimed *Hamlet*, Welles – still 16 – claimed to feel under-appreciated. They wouldn't give him Othello.

Welles left the Gate in March 1932, hoping to capitalise on his critical success in London or New York. But he couldn't get a work permit for England and his arrival in Manhattan was not the triumph he anticipated. Welles found few agents or companies – all struggling with the effects of the Depression – willing to give an unknown adolescent the time of day, even if he did have that cutting from the *Times*. Esteemed producers the Shuberts wouldn't even see him – worst of all, the assistant called him 'kiddie'!

Disappointed that, for all his accomplishments, his 10 months away had not made a star of him, Orson returned to the Midwest to be worshipped by Dadda and Skipper. Introducing a radio play years later, Welles intoned that *no man can explain the mystery and misery of being 17, that period which is almost a full stop in the involved sentence of a man's life, when every man's universe has growing pains and every man is his own Hamlet.*[26] Skipper did his best to spark Welles out of this fug, hiring him as Todd's drama coach. (Orson's *Twelfth Night*, whose dress rehearsal he recorded on film, won the Drama League cup.) Skipper also suggested that they should collaborate on a play about the abolitionist John Brown. Working in the peaceful environs of a Native American reservation, Welles conceived an ambitious work exploring the tensions between Brown's private self and public profile. *Marching Song's* opening scenes feature extensive argument and discussion of its central character so that his ultimate appearance is loaded with expectation. This would become a typical Wellesian trope: he strove to avoid in art and life the unheralded arrivals to which he had been subjected in Dublin and New York, cultivating for himself and his characters a reputation and mystique that ensured they could not be ignored by those around them.

Orson conceived other works on the reservation, expressing a more troubled side of his adolescence. *The Dark Room* was a melodrama set around a sèance; its climax – in which, *for the last time, the lights go out and The Voice speaks*[28] – harks back to Orson's impression of his dying mother

The old star actors never liked to come on until the end of the first act. Mister Wu is a classic example . . . All the other actors boil around the stage for about an hour shrieking, 'What will happen when Mister Wu arrives?', 'What is he like, this Mister Wu?' and so on. Finally a great gong is beaten, and slowly over a Chinese bridge comes Mister Wu himself . . . Peach Blossom (or whatever her name is) falls on her face and a lot of coolies yell, 'Mr Wu!!!' The curtain comes down, the audience goes wild, and everybody says, 'Isn't that guy playing Mister Wu a great actor!'[27]

speaking from the shadows and forward to Welles's radio career. *Bright Lucifer*, meanwhile, centres on an unavoidably autobiographical figure, a charismatic young egotist named Eldred Brand who – after another much-anticipated entry – sows division between his guardian Bill and Bill's brother Jack, a horror movie star. The talk is of make-up and magic, virgins and Hollywood; there is bitter argument over where affections lie, whom this *adopted orphan . . . as old as Egypt, this busy little bitch boy*[29] should love, who should love him – and how. (There are nakedly homoerotic undercurrents.) *Bright Lucifer* reaches a satanic crescendo; Eldred's death comes as a relief. The play was incomplete and perhaps not for public consumption anyway. For *Marching Song*, though, Welles and Skipper took a suite at the Algonquin in New York in full expectation of fielding offers. There were none. The chance of some radio work, briefly offered by a contact of Dadda's, fell through even before the 17-year-old's terms – $300 a week and billing as 'the internationally famous actor, Mr Orson Welles'[30] – could be rejected.

Another idea of Skipper's caught Orson's imagination: *Everybody's Shakespeare* would be a series of teaching editions introduced by Hill, illustrated by Welles and edited for performance by both. The aim was to cut through the intimidating aura of cultural elitism generally associated with the works, to establish them as living, humanist texts. Wanting to work away from distraction, Orson departed for Morocco. Even a conventional tourist visit in 1933 would have been challenging for a lone adolescent, but Welles claimed to have ventured into the little-known interior, reaching the court of the tribal leader Thami el Glaoui. A figure of tremendous tribal clout, Welles exaggerated only slightly in saying that el Glaoui *had killed one of his sons with a bow-string but he also knew how to sit in the Ritz Hotel and chat it up with Claudel*[31] – a role model for the savage sophisticates Welles would often play. Over the summer Orson made his way up to Seville, where he reported taking rooms above a brothel in the gypsy quarter, chipping away at *Everybody's Shakespeare* and trying his hand at pulp fiction and bullfighting – both of which would prove enduring interests.

Back in the US, he completed *Everybody's Shakespeare*, providing detailed stage directions and hundreds of accomplished illustrations for *Twelfth Night*, *The Merchant of Venice* and *Julius Caesar*. Set designs and staging plans ranged from impressionistic doodles to technically precise layouts; character sketches included broad cartoons and fine likenesses of specific actors. Shakespeare's language, Orson's essay on staging insisted, is *starlight and fireflies and the sun and the moon. He wrote it with tears and blood and beer, and his words march like heartbeats.*[32] Published the following year on the Todd Press, the books' combination of Hill's unstuffy enthusiasm, Welles's acute, well-informed stage sense and both men's lively, vivid prose attracted critical praise, a store-front display in Chicago and a publishing deal with Harpers. Suffused with Orson's conception of Shakespeare's plays as fast-paced, emotionally intense dramas with universal relevance, *Everybody's Shakespeare* did more to promote the works to schoolchildren than any other edition of the time, or for decades to come. The series remained in print for half a century.

Meanwhile Dadda and Skipper's contacts bore fruit: recognised by the playwright Thornton Wilder at a party in New York, Orson was subsequently introduced to Alexander Woollcott, a formidable critic who specialised in building (and destroying) reputations. That autumn Woollcott ensured that Welles was aesthetically and socially cultivated into a young man to watch. He was duly recruited into the most famous and successful theatrical company of the day – led by actor Katharine Cornell and director Guthrie McClintic – on no more than a nod from his new patrons. *Looks pretty much like the saga has begun,*[33] he wrote to Skipper as Cornell and McClintic prepped their new tour. Orson was disappointed to be cast as waif-like young men in *Candida* and *The Barretts of Wimpole Street*, and proved less than dedicated in rehearsals. McClintic and Cornell's respectful, conscientious approach to playmaking was almost the opposite of Welles's. The third production, however, was *Romeo and Juliet*, where his ease with the text set him apart from McClintic and Cornell, who were as daunted by Shakespeare as most producers, audiences and students of the time. As Mercutio, Orson gave a lusty performance at odds with 42-year-old Basil Rathbone's chilly Romeo. The critics loved it: the *Chicago Tribune* called him the 'Wonder Boy of Acting' and the *New York Times* gave a full-page rundown of the prodigy's heroic career (based, presumably, on his own or Dadda's decidedly heightened account). The seven-month tour provided Orson with opportunities to study every aspect of stagecraft, if not professionalism: his predilection for practical jokes irked his masters, prompting maudlin, heel-kicking apologies.

The tour did not satisfy McClintic and Cornell or their audiences and, to Welles's dismay, the Broadway opening was put on ice. In New York he picked up the first of his radio work at CBS, where he struck up a friendship with a young actor ten years his senior called Joseph Cotten. Meanwhile Orson and Skipper had conceived a combined Woodstock drama festival and Todd Theater Summer School – an opportunity to promote the school and, more importantly, Welles. Local critics were enlisted as advisors and, for a mere $250, students could learn the craft under

Orson's command. The Gate Theatre's Mac Liammóir and Edwards were sufficiently flattered and intrigued to agree to come over from Dublin and direct a play each. (Orson would handle the third.) Welles greeted them at the quay in New York with a gaggle of photographers.

Edwards chose *Tsar Paul*, which had a suitable part for Orson, a middle-aged heavy role, but one that required him to act rather than declaim. Mac Liammóir presented his *Hamlet*, with Welles as the Ghost again, and now Claudius as well, his make-up 'somewhere between an obscene old woman and the mask of lechery.'[35] Orson directed *Trilby*, playing that villainous master of suggestion, the hypnotist Svengali. His pantomime performance was pegged on a colossal proboscis that received more attention from Welles than his performance; when it melted in the dressing room after a fan was switched off, a roar of *Who ruined my nose?*[36] shook the building. Insecure about his own button nose, Welles was to construct prosthetics for almost every performance of his career, providing character definition and supplying (critic André Bazin has suggested) 'the need of a mask, that little shield of cardboard or modelling paste which suffices to defend you from the public. Acting with an exposed nose is like approaching the footlights naked.'[37]

Among the students enrolled on the course was a slender, blonde 18-year-old named Virginia Nicolson. Somewhat aristocratic with a provocative imagination, she and Orson were soon an item. With another student the couple collaborated on a short film, *The Hearts of Age* – Welles's debut as a film director. A pastiche of surrealist and expressionist films he had seen in New York (such as *Un Chien Andalou* and *The Cabinet of Dr Caligari*), it starred Orson as a heavily made-up death figure visiting an old woman, played by Virginia. Featuring cardboard gravestones and guttering candles, leering close-ups and arresting compositions, it also showed an ambitious, experimental approach to editing and processing.

Meanwhile the media charm offensive paid off and the Woodstock festival became that summer's destination for fashionable Chicagoans. As well as providing a return on Skipper's investment – a financial gamble whose stakes were higher than Orson's cavalier attitude suggested – the season's success ensured further press coverage for Welles. Around this time, McClintic and Cornell confirmed that their production of *Romeo and Juliet* would open on Broadway in a slimmed-down, speeded-up version closer to Welles's own ideas about Shakespeare. Unfortunately for Orson, the new lead in one of the other plays, Brian Aherne, had been given Mercutio. Welles now had the smaller role of Tybalt, though at least his slaying of Mercutio provided an opportunity to vent his bitterness in rehearsal: Aherne felt the duels were conducted 'with unnecessary venom . . . twice he broke my property sword off at the hilt.'[38] Orson also threw tantrums and rowed with McClintic, though his mood improved somewhat when Virginia joined him in New York. Realising their liaison would attract

Orson and Virginia Welles shortly after their wedding

unwanted attention they married without fuss on 14 November. *We really only got married in order to live together. It wasn't taken very seriously by either of us,*[39] maintained Welles, who may have been seeing other girls at the same time – he certainly saw little connection between marriage and monogamy, then or later. Virginia's parents were less blasé and insisted on a second, public ceremony, at which Dadda was best man.

On 20 December 1934, Orson Welles finally appeared before a Broadway audience. Auspiciously, it was a vocal debut: as well as Tybalt he was given the prologue, which he read masked. So the audience's first experience of Welles was of that rich voice in storytelling mode, inviting them to share the tale while prophesying its outcome. His prince of cats, meanwhile, was all hiss and scratch. One member of the second night audience was astonished to see 'death, in scarlet and black, in the form of a monstrous boy . . . What made this figure so obscene and terrible was the pale, shiny child's face under the unnatural growth of dark beard, from which there issued a voice of such clarity and power that it tore through the genteel, modulated voices of the well-trained professionals around him.'[40] The production was a great success, in which Welles, still seething over his demotion, was loath to share; he was even reluctant to take a curtain call. Orson's mood would change, and the real adventure begin, when that astonished second-night witness came to visit him backstage a few weeks later. His name was John Houseman.

The fall of the city, or Orson eats the Big Apple 1934–37

Another master of self-reinvention, John Houseman was born Jacques Haussman, a European Jew of mixed ancestry; relocating to the US, he had become a successful grain merchant by his mid-20s and now, at 33, was tentatively edging into the arts. Orson's explosive Tybalt played on his mind 'as a man nurtures his sense of excited anticipation over a woman the sight of whom has deeply disturbed him.'[41] Three weeks later, he knocked on Welles's dressing room door and invited the half-smiling, half-naked youth he found there for a drink; at the bar, the youngster's voice 'made people turn at neighbouring tables.'[42] The surprise was Orson's gentle, almost modest tone. Like other men before him, Houseman was utterly helpless when this glorious, preening lion cub rolled over and offered his belly. He felt lucky to be able to help; an occasional scratch from a playfully bared claw may even have added to the allure.

Their relationship moved from flirtation to action when Houseman offered Welles the lead in a play he was producing, Archibald MacLeish's *Panic*, an overcooked study of the ruin of a Wall Street colossus. Again, teenaged Orson seemed natural casting for a middle-aged autocrat. Welles later cited *Panic* as his introduction to progressive politics, but at the time he seemed merely to resent anything that distracted from his first Broadway lead: he heckled the intellectual symposium that followed the last night and was ejected from the theatre. Still, the critics liked him, so the collaboration was judged a success.

Meanwhile Orson's radio career was taking off. The Depression had seen wireless audiences boom and Welles was soon making a name for himself in a relatively small field. As well as contributing to documentaries, dramatisations and adaptations, he performed a scene from *Panic* on the news reconstruction magazine *The March of Time*, leading to regular cast membership. Radio proved the ideal medium for the

Welles works the microphone

mercurial young actor, providing a regular stream of new material without the need for tiresome rehearsals or memorising lines, and exploiting his remarkable vocal dexterity. A radio audience might be 60 million strong but it came in groups of two or three, so Orson could deploy the uncanny knack of conversational intimacy that served him so well in life. On stage he had to project and boom to overwhelm his audience; the microphone he could cradle and seduce.

Following *Panic*, Welles dazzled Houseman with plans 'to expose the anaemic elegance of Guthrie McClintic's *Romeo and Juliet* through an Elizabethan production of such energy and violence as New York had never seen.'[43] Like Orson and Skipper Hill's textbooks, this full-blooded thrill ride would reveal the dramatic heart of Renaissance drama. It was an ambitious plan, alien to both of the favoured theatrical styles of the day – social realism and escapist frippery – but the opportunity to realise it arose later that year, 1935. Houseman – who had previously

The Wall Street Crash of 1929 and the Great Depression that lasted throughout the following decade formed the most formidable crisis the US had faced since the Civil War. In 1935 President Franklin Roosevelt ordered the creation of a Works Progress Administration to create jobs and stimulate the economy. Most of the jobs were in public works but departments included the Federal Art Project, Federal Writers' Project and Federal Theatre Project. The WPA employed over 8 million people from its creation to its disbandment in 1943 following increasing right-wing opposition and the mass mobilisation of the population in wartime.

produced one of the mainstream American stage's few all-black productions – was asked to help run Harlem's Negro Theater Project, a part of the Federal Theatre Project (FTP). Houseman divided the project into a unit dealing with black issues and one presenting classical works and for the latter he enlisted lighting pioneer Abe Feder, accomplished musical director Virgil Thomson (both veterans of *Panic*) and, as director, Orson Welles.

Virginia had the bright idea of a *Macbeth* set in 19th-century Haiti, a country whose voodoo traditions would accommodate the play's supernatural elements.

Welles applied the same editorial ruthlessness he had displayed as a schoolboy dramaturge, chopping and shaping the play around his vision. His single set was a castle in a monstrous jungle; the colour and lighting would reflect the emotional ebb and flow of the action while constant background music – including a dozen genuine voodoo drummers – helped the novice actors' words *march like heartbeats*. Houseman, meanwhile, contributed artistic savoir-faire, business acumen and familiarity with FTP procedure – bureaucratic and diplomatic skills for which Welles, happy to bypass red tape by funnelling his own radio income into the production, had little respect.

So while most Americans, including those in New York's entertainment industry, were struggling to put food on the table, this untried 20-year-old director was earning $1,000 a week on the radio and – thanks to anti-Depression measures – about to mount a well-resourced Broadway production of his choosing. Unemployed? *I was so employed I forgot how to sleep.*[44] Welles rushed from his radio day jobs to nocturnal rehearsals, after which he regularly made the most of Harlem nightlife in the company of his Macbeth, Jack Carter. An alcoholic convicted killer with mob connections, Carter was a striking, charismatic figure whose presence fuelled the gossip surrounding the already-controversial production. Perhaps justifiably, many in Harlem suspected the production would be sensationalist or exploitative and Orson was lucky to avoid serious injury from a razor attack.

The opening night, 14 April 1936, was a frenzy of anticipation: four city blocks had to be sealed off and the curtain went up an hour late. The play opened with voices in the darkness, chanting ominously to the drums, before the witch doctors, sumptuous balls, military tattoos, masks, costumes, writhing half-naked bodies, bullwhips, gunshots and headlong tumbles worked their magic. The audience was ecstatic, the cast (and Welles) took several beaming curtain calls and the critics were breathless – even if they weren't all convinced that breathlessness alone signified a great production. But Welles had made an African-American production impossible to ignore – *Macbeth* transferred to Broadway for two months then went on tour, playing to 117,244 people – and proved the sceptics wrong. *I had conquered Harlem! I would go up two or three nights a week to Harlem where I was the king. I really was the king!*[45]

The voodoo *Macbeth* provided triumphant validation of Welles and Houseman's collaboration, but the seeds of its breakdown were already present. Houseman saw in Welles both bold creativity and the self-assurance to put it into effect, while Orson recognised the value of his partner's cool, pragmatic judgment. Neither could have accomplished alone what their partnership made possible, and each resented it. To Welles in particular, the idea of another person being indispensable to his success was infuriating. He insisted on full credit for the production, instigating a furious row when the *New York Times* attributed it to Houseman too. Throughout his early career, Welles trumpeted his sole responsibility for works undertaken in the inherently collaborative media of theatre, radio and film. Such were the demands of his image as 'Orson Welles, Boy Wonder'. But his true genius was less for creating things from scratch than using his vision and charisma to adapt, synthesise, catalyse and galvanise his own and others' work into something beyond the capacity of any single contributor.

Being conquered, Harlem lost its allure for Orson, and the Negro Theater Project with it. Houseman negotiated the creation of an FTP classical unit – known by its federal denomination, Project 891 – and a home for it, the Maxine Elliott theatre. He and Welles recruited a number of the latter's accomplished radio colleagues, including Joseph Cotten (FTP regulations permitted a 10 per cent quota of working professionals alongside those on work relief). Many of the remaining performers were unemployed former vaudevillians and showgirls, and the opening production – *Horse Eats Hat*, a loose adaptation of Eugène Labiche's 1851 farce *An Italian Straw Hat* – provided ample opportunity for the exercise of their variety of skills. Around the get-me-to-the-church-on-time plot, Welles, Edwin Denby and Virgil Thomson created a radically playful formal experiment in which the production itself was as precarious as the story: scenery collapsed, performers dangled from chandeliers and the whole thing seemed on the brink of glorious self-destruction. By apparently letting the audience in on the trick, he in fact pulled off a larger illusion.

Following Project 891's successful first production, both Welles and Houseman took on work outside the unit. However, neither the Broadway play in which Orson took the lead nor the *Hamlet* directed by Houseman proved a success and both returned to 891, mildly shamefaced at their co-dependence. For their next collaboration, they decided on another Renaissance tragedy of supernatural horror, *Doctor Faustus*. Not only did Orson's expansive style suit Marlowe's brash overreacher to a tee but *Faustus* was the conjuror's play to end them all. Welles, a keen amateur magician since childhood, conceived a now-you-see-it-now-you-don't production set on a dark, bare stage whose concealed trapdoors and tubes and cones covered in black velvet combined with state-of-the-art lighting to make characters appear, disappear or even levitate. Lighting director Abe Feder provided bright walls and columns in the air: 'light itself was to take the place of the object that was to be illuminated'[46]. The audience would again be initiated by a prologue incanted in darkness and, excited by the dramatic possibilities of his day job on the air, Welles had voices and sound effects broadcast to the auditorium from 'hell'. Nor was his infatuation with radio merely aesthetic: he described his *use of the radio method of directing . . . Whenever I wanted anything or anybody, I spoke into a microphone, and my voice reached the remotest parts of the building. People came running as if they had heard Gabriel blowing his trumpet.*[47] There's a dangerous idea of divinity in that, a blithe faith in the potency of one's own voice that would undo not just Faustus but many of Welles's later filmic incarnations. But how could Orson's head not swell when awestruck headlines hailed him as 'Actor, Writer, Director and Not Quite 22', and when the critics anointed *Faustus* the FTP's 'principal artistic achievement'[48] and asked if its director shouldn't head a National Theater?

Orson's radio work, from poetry readings to commercials, continued to proliferate. Most impressive was his landing the plum role of the Shadow in CBS's revamped top-rated mystery series. Now the lead character as well as narrator of the series, the Shadow – a mysterious crime-fighter known by day as suave socialite Lamont Cranston – was able to cloud men's minds into thinking him invisible. He was 'never seen, only heard'[49], an

Although radio had been developing as a broadcast medium since the end of World War One, it was only in the late 1920s, with the consolidation of national networks NBC and CBS, that it took hold as a means of mass communication. By the end of the 1930s an estimated 90 per cent of American homes had radios. Supplying the entire continent with live news and musical and comedy entertainment, radio helped both to inform the population and to strengthen national identity. President Roosevelt proved a canny exploiter of the medium's potential for intimacy with his famously reassuring 'fireside chats'.

ominous voice in the darkness, an ideal Welles vehicle and a personification of radio itself. Episode titles included 'The Phantom Voice', 'The Voice of Death', and 'The Hypnotised Audience', in which Orson undid a dastardly swami's spell by crying out, 'Stop! Everyone listen to me!' He also narrated *Panic* author Archibald MacLeish's new radio play *The Fall of the City*, about the arrival of an armoured conqueror before whose iconic appeal the populace fall prostrate. Yet when he lifts his visor, 'the helmet is hollow. The metal is empty, the armor is empty. I tell you there is no one at all there.'

The Shadow was soon the smash show of the season and Welles lived high on the hog. He and Virginia had a lavish lakeside home outside the city at Sneden's Landing and each morning Orson would take a motorboat across the water to his limo. Once in town he'd have his shave and manicure, enjoy a swanky lunch and then shuttle between his various commitments in an ambulance he had procured for the purpose, sirens blaring.

Early in 1937, Welles met the composer Marc Blitzstein, whose new 'people's opera' *The Cradle Will Rock* became 891's next project. Blitzstein had been a musical prodigy and studied with Schoenberg. A charismatic, intense character, he was a committed Marxist and had created an allegorical fable in which the workers of Steeltown, USA, rise against their boss and his whorish lackeys. The score, influenced by Brecht and Weill, also employed jazz, gospel and classical music, and the opera's single 90-minute act suited Welles's preference for short shows with no intervals. Orson was by now a political progressive and resolutely anti-fascist; though he was not a communist sympathiser, he found himself drawn to Blitzstein's political zeal. For his part, Blitzstein allowed himself to be won over to Welles's decidedly un-Brechtian vision of a glitzy production with a highly stylised coloured-glass set. The usual regimen of nocturnal rehearsals got underway.

Conservative criticism of the Works Progress Administration's leftist agenda had been growing over the past year, and industrial unrest was turning ugly, especially in the steel industry. The right pounced on the news that the FTP was preparing to stage a pro-union play with federal funds. At the same time, 7,000 WPA members went on strike over proposed cuts to the FTP. On 10 June the federal government slashed the FTP budget by 30 per cent and put all new productions on hold until 1 July – two weeks after *Cradle* was scheduled to open. Orson was uncertain what to do. He was reluctant to suspend the show but hesitant to martyr himself for a cause that wasn't really his. But when federal guards sealed the Maxine Elliott theatre in advance of a preview performance in front of an invited audience, Welles decided there was no room for nego-tiation. *I thought if you padlock a theater, he recalled, then the argument is closed. [Otherwise] I would never have taken that strong a stand.*[50] Some argued that to go ahead with the production would be needlessly provocative, leaving an already-vulnerable FTP subject to further attack. But Orson decided the show must go on.

Word got around that the search was on for a new venue. Project 891's attorney Arnold Weissberger had advised that any non-feder-al property was acceptable, but the performers could not appear on stage without jeopardising their right to vital union benefits. Deprived of their elaborate glass sets and complex lighting, Welles and Houseman gained access to the Venice Theater hours before the 16 June premiere was scheduled to go on. They redirected the audience uptown, still uncertain of being able to deliver the show. Now 'trapped in the role of hero'[51] Orson was at the epicentre of something more than a play. Once the audience was seated, he used his radio skills to describe to the packed house the production they couldn't see. Blitzstein nervously started to play the piano. One by one, the cast members – about half of them – piped up from their places among the audience. By singing from the stalls they adhered to union rules while adding an improvisatory frisson, enhanced by the frequent failure of the single spotlight to find them while they sang. Their voices made the darkness dangerous, alive, as if the audience were possessed by the play.

Orson knew he had presided over another triumph – the papers were full of it. He must have felt more potent than ever; at any rate, his first child was born to Virginia exactly nine months later (at no apparent cost to his ongoing extra-marital activities – ballerinas were his latest fixation). A recreation of that exhilarating first night ran at the Venice for a fortnight – a decision motivated, the press were told, by 'good showmanship.'[52] The day after the sensational first performance, Orson flew to Washington to justify his actions to the WPA top brass. He had no time for their argument that, whatever his production's merits – and these were never called into doubt – by breaking ranks Orson could only have weakened the position of the FTP and WPA as a whole. But Welles never gave much thought to the larger concerns that might underpin an organisation whose resources were at his disposal. The FTP was indeed extinct a couple of years later. The effects on Project 891 were more immediate: the authorities smashed *Cradle*'s scenery, Welles resigned and Houseman was sacked under new regulations barring foreign nationals from the FTP. The project was over, its other members – like so many of Welles's junior collaborators – left blinking in the settling dust, like rabbits left on stage after the magician vanishes.

Mercury Rising 1937–39

Project 891 was dead. Long live the Mercury Theater! Welles and Houseman enjoyed a brief break over summer 1937: there was, the latter recalled, 'the usual need . . . to prove that each of us could exist without the other',[53] so he pursued academic opportunities while Welles delivered the first radio project over which he had creative control. A ratings success as The Shadow as well as a theatrical *wunderkind*, Orson was a natural choice to create a prestige series, a non-commercial programme designed to boost the networks' reputation with low financial stakes. The Mutual network offered him carte blanche to write, produce, direct and star in a project of his choice and, rather than the more usual adaptations of films or plays, Orson conceived a six-part version of *Les Misérables*. The crew included experienced professionals and the cast was drawn from Orson's radio and stage collaborators (Virginia played his surrogate daughter) but the only name credited to listeners was Orson Welles. It was a strikingly novel production, as dramatically compulsive as it was aurally rich. As well as giving unusual prominence to the narrator's role (which Welles of course played, as well as the lead Jean Valjean), it made bold use of sound design – the chase through the sewers, for instance, was recorded over a urinal.

By August Welles and Houseman were back together, making plans for a brand new company. They chose the name Mercury – with its intimations of fleet-footed adaptability, important tidings and alchemist's quicksilver – and, on 29 August 1937, published a declaration of principles on the front page of the *New York Times* drama section. Like 891, the Mercury would deliver accessible classics and exciting new works at low prices; it would be socially conscious but artistic concerns came first. These lofty pronouncements came before funding was secured – just as, once a theatre was found, the neon 'Mercury' sign was fixed before the heating or seating. But the pair soon found supporters to put their money where Orson's mouth was and 3,000 actors applied for the three dozen acting positions, most of which went to long-standing collaborators like Joseph Cotten, George Coulouris and the comic Chubby Sherman.

Welles photographed by Cecil Beaton on the set of *Julius Caesar*

Their first production was a pared-down modern-dress *Julius Caesar* subtitled 'Death of a Dictator', set in a contemporary Fascist regime. Featuring ramps and platforms against brick, the set was simple but capable of spectacular effects. Welles composed scenes like movie shots and continued in his use of expressionistic lighting effects, throwing great beams of light upward as if in mimicry of the Nuremberg rallies. The complex soundtrack of jackboots and a volatile mob proved too much for the speaker system, but was rich enough to make this the first stage production released as an LP. Welles was to play Brutus, conceived as *the eternal, impotent, ineffectual, fumbling liberal*.[54] As director, however, Orson was nothing if not dictatorial, perched on a high stool in the pit with his microphone. He had food brought in ('oysters and champagne, red meat and burgundy, dessert and brandy'[55] was a typical night's fare) and 'approached other talents as he did his gargantuan meals,' according to technical director Jean Rosenthal. 'Your contributions to his feast he either spat out or set aside untouched, or he ate them up . . . with a gusto which was extraordinarily flattering.'[56]

Regularly working up to 20 hours a day between stage and radio, Orson's infectious energy compensated for his directorial haranguing and frequent rows with Houseman. (Welles fostered the latter's starchy, interfering reputation within the company even while depending on his administrative and critical nous more than ever.) Not all were won over, especially when Houseman informed them that 'it was important that Orson be given sole credit for everything.'[57] The team threatened to walk out over pay and conditions, and Welles's approach to his role impressed no one: having reshaped the play around Brutus, he barely learned his lines or appeared on stage before the dress rehearsal, concentrating his perfectionism on continual changes to the blocking of key scenes. The dress was disastrous and Orson made further drastic changes. When the lights went down for the

Unused scene from the *Citizen Kane* script: newspaper tycoon Kane is talking to the 'nervous and harassed' foreman of one of his papers.

KANE *(turning to* SMATHERS, *quietly): Let's do these pages over again . . .*
SMATHERS: *We go to press in five minutes. We can't remake them, Mr Kane.*
KANE *reaches out and shoves the forms onto the floor, where they scatter into hundreds of bits.*
KANE: You can remake them now, can't you, Mr Smathers?[58]

first night – even the exit lights were extinguished, against fire regulations, for the sake of that first voice in the darkness – the production hung in the balance.

It was a sensation. The *New York Post* found it 'the most exciting, the most imaginative, the most topical, the most awesome, and the most absorbing'[59] production of the season. The critics favourably compared its sleek power, on a budget of just $6,000, to the stolid, monumental *Antony and Cleopatra* that had just failed on Broadway. ('$6,000?!' squawked its star, Tallulah Bankhead. 'That's less than one of my fucking breastplates!'[60]) There were questions over Orson's performance, and again over quite what it all *meant* – was the show itself more than flashy demagoguery? – but the Mercury had unquestionably delivered on its promise to offer something new, something unique.

Rather than capitalise on the success, Welles and Houseman kept prices low and turned to their next production. Rehearsals were soon underway for John Ford's city comedy *The Shoemaker's Holiday* (1600). With stylised period settings and huge codpieces, it was as light as *Caesar* was grave. On Christmas Eve 1937, Orson invited the *Caesar* audience to stay put for a preview, conspiratorially changing the set before their eyes like a conjuror showing he has nothing up his sleeves. As one report put it, 'The audience felt intimately connected with the actors when they heard calls of 'Is everybody ready?' 'Places please!' and 'All right, let her up, boys!' But if only they had known that even these yells had been rehearsed with the cast earlier that evening, line for line.

Quite a showman, Mr Welles.'[61] By New Year's Day 1938, *Shoemaker* was running successfully, *The Cradle Will Rock* was playing in rep (advertised as 'THE SHOW THAT MADE THE FRONT PAGES'[62]) and *Caesar* was on tour. The Mercury was the toast of Broadway – yet its low admission prices barely met its overheads.

Chubby Sherman meanwhile had noted that 'all our plays so far have been in the manner of stunts, and some day we'll be producing a real play in which an actor opens a door, a real door, walks in, sits down and begins to talk. And that'll be the end of us!'[63] And so they came to George Bernard Shaw's *Heartbreak House*. The rights were expensive and Shaw, unswayed by the Welles legend, forbade editorial changes. Denied his customary directorial latitude, Orson's attentions went into designing his make-up – the 22-year-old played 88-year-old Captain Shotover – and quelling the growing rumblings from his company. *I am the Mercury Theatre*[64] was his imperious conclusion to one crisis meeting.

Orson and Virginia's daughter was delivered on 27 March and given a boy's name, apparently for the sake of an arrestingly phrased telegram: *Christopher, she is born.* But Welles had higher priorities than fatherhood. The Mercury's funds continued to dwindle and Sherman left the company, scuppering plans for *The Importance of Being Earnest.* Welles reeled from what he took as a personal betrayal, but to the outside world he remained on top: the cover of *Time* magazine a few weeks later featured Orson

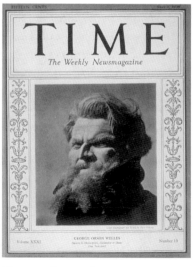

News on the march

as Shotover looking like God. The spread, headed 'Marvelous Boy', noted that 'he loves the mounting Welles legend, but wants to keep the record straight'[65], half of which was true. *Heartbreak House* opened to muted if constructive reviews; ticket sales, however, were not great. At the end of its first season, the Mercury had made a tremendous splash, but what would remain after the ripples dispersed? And why was Orson giving speeches disparaging the theatre as an art form?

Part of the reason could have been CBS's recent offer to the Mercury of a run of radio shows. The network was keen to enhance its image by commissioning a long-running artistically credible series and Welles, having proved himself with *Les Misérables* and now appearing on the cover of *Time*, was a cinch for the job. Subtitled *First Person Singular*, the *Mercury Theatre on the Air* would present adaptations of classic stories – not plays or films – with Orson as narrator and lead. Radio, he explained, *demands a form impossible to the stage. The images called up by a broadcast must be imagined, not seen . . . radio drama is more akin to the form of the novel, to story telling, than to anything else . . . Radio's particular amendment is the personalising of Chorus, of making him a character in the play instead of an outside character looking in.*[66] Thus Orson would dip in and out of the action, exploiting his knack for suggesting intimacy with millions at once. A number of Mercury stalwarts, including Houseman, now Welles's subordinate for the first time, joined him in the venture. The company spent three weeks developing *Treasure Island* as the inaugural show but a couple of days before the transmission date of 11 July 1938, Orson changed it to *Dracula* (perhaps for the echoes of the Shadow?) and achieved another seat-of-his-pants success.

The next two months' productions included that *Treasure Island*, stories by Dickens and Schnitzler ('we all play parts; happy is he that knows it'), and a life of Lincoln. The final show was Welles's own adaptation of G K Chesterton's *The Man Who Was*

Thursday, a baroque, self-consuming detective thriller of the type that came to characterise his filmography. Despite his billing – 'written, directed, produced and performed by Orson Welles' – the star usually only became involved once the show had been adapted and rehearsed. Having listened to a recording, he would make changes and orchestrate the live performance from his microphone podium like a conductor. The contributions of Houseman, producer Paul Stewart and the remarkable young composer Bernard Herrmann (who would later create the scores for *Citizen Kane*, *Psycho*, *Taxi Driver* and many others) were indispensable, but without Welles's insistence on experimentation and perfectionism the shows could not have succeeded as they did.

Welles and Houseman were also planning the Mercury's new theatre season, offering the now-familiar combination of knock-about comedy, political allegory and Shakespearean verve. First up was a farce, *Too Much Johnson*, due to open in Connecticut on 16 August en route to Broadway. Orson took the production as an excuse to experiment with film: having shown an interest in cinematic staging and lighting in *Faustus* and *Caesar*, Welles now decided to substitute an actual movie for the expository scenes of all three acts. Having studied the great silent comedians, he spent 10 days – and most of the Mercury's paltry resources – staging a suffragette march, a cliff-top duel and Joseph Cotten's two-storey leap into a cabbage cart. Working on the footage in his quarters at the St Regis Hotel, Welles began his life-long love affair with editing, which allowed him the godlike control over his material that his human colleagues sometimes resisted. In the meantime he neglected the rehearsals of the live performances. Then it became clear that the Connecticut theatre was incapable of running the movie, and rights issues prevented it being shown in New York anyway. The whole production was dead in the water and Orson's first sustained experiment in film became his first unfinished picture.

Devastated by the failure, Welles took to his bed for a week, 'convinced that he was going to die, racked by asthma, fear and despair,'[67] in Houseman's recollection. Orson had suffered depressions before in times of distress, but he usually followed them soon after with bouts of extreme industry. This time, however, his will seemed more seriously weakened. In his next production – *Danton's Death*, Georg Büchner's tragedy of the French Revolution – he opted for a role 'in which he could be replaced without damage' and his editing of the problematic play was quixotic and subject to constant change. The set, dominated by a teetering staircase, catwalks and an elevator shaft, was a deathtrap – actor Erskine Sanford broke his leg – and rehearsals were unfocused and increasingly ill-tempered. There were problems with costumes, lighting and the operation of the technically complex set; even the one potential *coup de theatre*, a cyclorama of 1,400 Halloween masks intended to represent the mob, the Revolutionary tribunal and the dead, wouldn't work. Houseman thought it the first time Welles had lacked a driving vision of a production.

A more fruitful outlet for Welles's creative frenzies – and the exercise of his persecution complex – came from the radio show, with its short deadlines and behind-closed-doors performance. (Orson refused to have a studio audience: one of the pleasures of radio was the one-way interaction with listeners.) 'Sweating, howling, dishevelled and singlehanded he wrestled with chaos and time,' Houseman wrote, 'always conveying an effect of being alone, traduced by his collaborators, surrounded by treachery, ignorance, sloth, indifference, incompetence and . . . downright sabotage.'[68] After the successful trial period CBS had picked up the show for a 26-week run, but rescheduled it against the sensationally successful ventriloquist act of Edgar Bergen and Charlie McCarthy. The Mercury's presentations included their stage *Caesar*, and adaptations of *Jane Eyre* and *Around the*

World in 80 Days. Hopes were not high for the 30 October 1938 broadcast: Howard Koch's adaptation of H G Wells's *The War of the Worlds* was not considered particularly strong, but since *Danton's Death* opened just three days later, there was, for once, no time to reconsider.

Houseman had told Koch to relocate the story to contemporary America and use mock news reports to add punch. Faux reportage was familiar territory for Welles: news media had featured in *Marching Song* and a number of his stage and radio productions. The story got gently underway, with cod presentations of dance music interrupted by bulletins about disturbances on Mars and a meteorite in New Jersey. Things heated up just as Edgar Bergen's guest singer had millions switching over to try out the Mercury's latest offering.

Increasingly agitated reports of monsters and heat rays built to the apocalyptic scenario of New York levelled by giant robots and, finally, a quintessentially Wellesian sign of calamity and impotence: a lone voice calling futilely for acknowledgement across empty airwaves. After the break, Orson's character, an astronomer, narrated a more conventional account of the attack's aftermath and monsters' defeat, followed by a conventional sign-off and reminder that the story was a Halloween yarn. But by then the damage was done: almost one in five of

'Something's wriggling out of the shadow like a grey snake. Now it's another one, and another. They look like tentacles to me. There, I can see the thing's body. It's as large as a bear and it glistens like wet leather. But that face – it . . . ladies and gentlemen, it's indescribable. I can hardly force myself to keep looking at it, it's so awful. The eyes are black and gleam like a serpent. The mouth is kind of V-shaped with saliva dripping from its rimless lips that seem to quiver and pulsate . . . This is the most extraordinary experience. I can't find words . . . I'm pulling this microphone with me as I talk . . . Hold on, will you please, I'll be back in a minute. [Dead air]'

'CARL PHILIPS' DESCRIBES THE MARTIANS

the 9 million listeners are estimated to have believed the invasion was real. Roads, stations and switchboards were jammed from coast to coast (especially around New Jersey itself). In Harlem churches were heaving; in Alabama sorority girls queued tearfully for the phone to bid parents farewell; in Louisiana a Linotyper, fleeing through the night, caught his neck on a clothesline and thought he'd been struck by a death ray.

Welles wakes to find himself a sinner

The following morning the scare dominated the papers. Appearing ruffled after all-night rehearsals on *Danton's Death*, Welles offered his familiar brand of cap-wringing, while expressing amazement that anyone could have taken the show seriously. Orson seemed so tickled by the fiasco (even if he had not intended it) that it is difficult to take his apology entirely seriously. And although 'The War of the Worlds' had indeed been advertised, listed and introduced in the usual way, it was also the first Mercury broadcast set in contemporary America and the first not dominated by Orson's subjective narration. Some of the coverage of the scare called for tighter broadcasting controls (which were imposed), but much of it took listeners' credulity to task. As with the *Cradle Will Rock* controversy, Orson had presided over a sensational event not really of his design, and this one brought both international fame and a sponsor for the show (Campbell's Soup). Again the question of credit was raised, albeit discreetly: when, in 1940, a Princeton academic sent Welles the manuscript of his study of the scare, Orson was alarmed to find Howard Koch credited as the broadcast's writer and mounted an increasingly embittered defence of his own role. The book was published and Koch credited, to no discernible effect on Welles's reputation or career.

The Martian scandal raised Orson's profile immeasurably – 'any day now,' Houseman presumed, 'the offers from Hollywood would start arriving'[69] – but did little to help *Danton's Death*. It closed after 21 performances and reviews that found 'all technique and no drama; all switchboard and no soul.'[70] 'For the Mercury Theatre,' the *Herald Tribune* decreed, 'the honeymoon is over.'[71] The honeymoon proved to be all there was; Welles and Houseman lost the will and the Mercury effectively folded. As Houseman noted, 'Orson [was] becoming a great national figure . . . in almost exactly inverse proportion to the success of his artistic and professional endeavours.'[72] Most of the senior Mercury cast were still involved in the *Mercury Theater on the Air*, which became the *Campbell Playhouse* that December. The sponsors imposed a more populist agenda: Hollywood guest stars began appearing and Orson added celebrity chitchat to his ring-leading repertoire.

But there was one last theatrical project to be undertaken beneath the Mercury banner: the Shakespearean history digest that Welles had attempted at Todd and had spent the previous year reworking into a mammoth, unwieldy script known as *Five Kings*. On the basis of *Caesar*'s appeal to schoolchildren, the subscription-funded Theater Guild had pledged backing for an east coast tour and New York opening. Welles got to work revising his marathon script: he would play Falstaff, whom he viewed not as a bawdy, happy-go-lucky clown but an absurdist, even tragic character who uses his gift for entertainment for advantage and self-defence. The script still ran at over six hours and the technically-complex turntable set – which allowed characters to move from street to field to tavern with 'fadeouts, pan shots, dissolves and all the other tricks of the cinema'[73] – proved preposterously over-ambitious, especially for a tour with constantly changing venues. Orson was soon playing hooky from his own production, a rampant Falstaff indulging in food, drink and sex in the company of his Hal, Burgess Meredith. When present he told travelling anecdotes or threw tantrums. Relations with Houseman hit a new low and the opening night in Boston was mounted on the basis of an under-rehearsed, constantly changing script little understood by the cast, let alone audience. The critics were baffled or scathing – 'a non-sequitur de force,'[74] *Time* called it – and the script revisions continued.

During March 1939 it limped to Washington and Philadelphia, where the turntable had to be cranked by hand. Confronted with damning reviews, spiralling budgets and hotel bills for damaged chandeliers, the Guild put *Five Kings* on hold. In penance or defiance, Welles vowed not to shave off his Falstaff beard until the production was revived – which would happen, but not for two decades. This abortive tour, Houseman wrote, was like 'the terminal stages of a complicated and fatal disease. The name of our disease was success – accumulating success that had little to do with the quality of our work but seemed to proliferate around the person of Orson Welles with a wild, monstrous growth of its own.'[75] This terrible image of fame as a cancer would only seem more prescient as Welles's career progressed.

For the time being it marked an unprecedented low point in a once-remarkable creative partnership now characterised by 'fatigue, humiliation, mutual reproaches.'[76] Orson's other marriage, to Virginia, had collapsed into divorce proceedings too. Rather than take to his bed in the midst of such artistic and personal disaster, Orson took to the comforts of vaudeville. He mounted a hammy version of William Archer's ludicrous melodrama *The Green Goddess*. The unprofitable presentation limped as far as Pittsburgh on the RKO vaudeville circuit before folding, but its prologue – a five-minute film montage – pointed the way to Orson's future. Houseman had been right: the movie offers were coming in.

Mr Genius comes through 1939–41

'Instead of having to make himself known and recognised
{on his arrival in Hollywood, Welles} found himself . . .
having to uphold a reputation that was already immense.'[77]

François Truffaut

The way he told it later, Welles fell into his theatrical and
movie careers without plan or ambition. Not so. His stage and
radio work had been noticed in Hollywood even before 'The War
of the Worlds' made him a hot property: he had turned down
character roles and an offer to head the powerful producer David
O Selznick's script department, explaining it wasn't *a step towards
my ultimate aim: my profession of actor-director*.[78] Orson had played
hard to get until finally – amazingly – he got what he wanted.
The Hollywood studio system was at its apex in the 1930s;
with a few hard-won exceptions the director was merely another
cog in the machine. When, on 22 July 1939, RKO's George
Schaefer handed Welles the contract that stunned Hollywood –
according to which Welles was to write, produce, direct and
star in two pictures – he was hardly ignorant of the impact it
would make. In fact the impact was the point: Schaefer was
buying Orson's image as much as his talent. Like CBS, RKO
was keen to develop inexpensive prestige projects and the man
behind both the Mercury Theatre and the Martian 'hoax' had a
proven knack for making a splash on the arts and the news pages.
Though Welles, as producer, had final cut, the studio had script

RKO, the first new studio of the sound era, emerged in 1928 from the merger of a studio, a radio corporation and a chain of vaudeville theatres. Notorious for its constantly changing bosses, the studio struggled to create a distinctive profile, but this resulted in a notably diverse output. After early hits such as Fred Astaire-Ginger Rogers musicals and *King Kong* (1933), the studio made screwball comedies (*Bringing Up Baby*, 1938) and, later, the Johnny Weissmuller *Tarzan* pictures, horror movies such as *Cat People* (1943) and dramas like *They Live By Night* (1947).

approval and the budget was nothing special. What was the worst that could happen?

To Orson the combination of carte blanche terms and the resources of a major institution was nothing new: the government had bankrolled his plays and CBS his radio work. To Hollywood, however, this 23-year-old – who blithely planned to knock off his first film by the end of the year and get back to Broadway – was the ungracious beneficiary of the most outrageous fortune. When he went out west that summer, still bearing his Falstaff beard, the boy wonder made little attempt to ingratiate himself with the locals and the luxurious lifestyle of the all-male Mercury ménage got tongues wagging – and, given the company's substantial debts, alarmed his lawyer and agent. A cowboy actor cut off Welles's tie in a restaurant, a song called 'Little Orson Annie' did the rounds, someone sent him a bearded ham in the mail. For the first time in his life, reputation and controversy were working against Welles's interests rather than promoting them.

Childishly excited at being gifted *the greatest electric train set a boy ever had*,[79] Orson didn't realise how suspicious it was in Hollywood to care more for movies than for money; to see them as an end rather than a means. Over the next couple of months he undertook a crash course from RKO's various departments. (He was especially delighted by the sound bank, with its full spectrum of weather effects and dozen different kisses.) For his own picture,

Welles planned to be 'actor director master of ceremonies and narrator . . . identical to his function on radio show'[80] – or so Houseman told the Campbell's Soup people in a cable. The second season of the radio show (still based in New York) was underway and although their theatrical partnership had ended, Houseman was still involved in Mercury work and had come west with Orson. He soon returned east, however, having struggled unsuccessfully to adapt Joseph Conrad's *Heart of Darkness* into a screenplay for Welles. The *Mercury Theatre on the Air* had performed a version of the story the previous year; framed in self-conscious narration, it was a natural choice for radio. Now Orson envisaged a film in the first person singular, shot entirely from the point of view of the narrator and with Orson appearing only as a voice. The prologue conceived to help acclimatise the audience to this novel approach was to start with a giant close-up of his mouth directly addressing them.

Orson shuttled between coasts to fulfil his weekly radio commitments (making him TWA's customer of the year) until in November the Mercury cast – including Joseph Cotten, Agnes Moorehead, Ray Collins and Everett Sloane – was shipped out west. There was by now growing friction with Campbell's over the artistic quality of the series: the sponsors' feedback on one show acknowledged that 'the atmosphere was stunning in its perfection, but there was too damn much of it.'[81]

Heart of Darkness soon ran into casting difficulties, while the war in Europe severely curtailed the prestige market Orson had been recruited to service. Scaling back, Welles continued work on the project but could not square his radically innovative viewpoint with the studio's. *Mine was taken to be ignorance, and I read their position as, you know, established dumbheadedness.*[82] Houseman wondered if Welles wasn't delaying because 'the moment it gets made it enters the world of tangible-work-to-be-appraised instead of potential-work-of-a-genius-which-can-be-talked-conjectured-about-written-about.'[83] By the end of November the film's budget had risen to over $1 million – double the expected cost – and Schaefer put it on indefinite hold: Orson's second unfinished film. Having expected to deliver a movie by New Year, Orson entered December with nothing to show for his famous contract but a bulging clippings file.

Bulging not least because of Orson's burgeoning romance with Dolores Del Rio, the Mexican screen siren who had first appeared on screen aged 20 in 1925; the adolescent Welles had lusted after her image in such films as *The Loves of Carmen* and *Bird of Paradise*. But there was a break-up too: during a dinner at Chasen's restaurant, Welles and Houseman had a furious row after the latter drew attention to the unpaid Mercury cast's continued inactivity. Orson, always quick to perceive betrayal, roared his fury and lobbed a lighted table heater towards his tormentor, prompting the curtains to catch light and Houseman to leave town. From New Mexico Houseman wrote a cordial letter of separation acknowledging that 'instead of being helpful and fruitful [the relationship] merely succeeds in embarrassing and paralysing us both.'[84]

Orson's financial situation was also a cause for concern. With the end of the *Campbell's Playhouse* run in March 1940, his income dried up and he embarked on a quick fund-raising lecture tour in advance of his 25th birthday in May, when his trust fund matured. In the event he was upset to find that only $2,692 of the $33,438 in his fund was left after taxes and debts were accounted for. (Is this the source of the long-running theme in his films of resentment of income tax?)

Orson had also been searching for a new film project. After considering a couple of thriller ideas, Welles had started collaborating with one of the writers from the radio show. Former *New Yorker* journalist Herman Mankiewicz had 15 years' service and some impressive titles on his Hollywood resumé, including several Marx Brothers films and newsroom comedies. Ferociously witty and intelligent, he was also a vituperatively bitter alcoholic whose unreliability made him all but unemployable, and something of a social pariah. ('It's all right, Arthur,' he told a notoriously punctilious host after vomiting at his table. 'The white wine came up with the fish.'[85]) Orson was delighted by this perennial outsider, who entertained him with stories of life at San Simeon, the palatial folly that was home to the press baron William Randolph Hearst and his mistress Marion Davies. The idea arose between them of writing a portrait of some comparable great American figure, told from a variety of perspectives. The precise origin of this conception remains contentious: the interest in reputation and narrative complexity is consistent with Welles's earlier work, while 'Mank' had developed other scripts about American giants. With his mischievous streak, Mank may already have realised that he had another subject, just as great as Hearst, under his nose: Houseman later acknowledged that they were 'creating a vehicle

William Randolph Hearst and Marion Davies at play

William Randolph Hearst (1863–1951), the son of a mining millionaire and senator, took over his father's *San Francisco Examiner* aged 23, soon making salacious 'yellow journalism' the basis of a national newspaper chain. Elected to the House of Representatives, he failed to become Mayor or Governor of New York, or secure the Democratic Presidential nomination. Despite remaining married to the mother of his five sons, Hearst fell in love with the talented comic actress Marion Davies and for three decades held court with her at San Simeon, his purpose-built California castle. His fortunes never fully recovered from the Wall Street crash.

for a man who at 24 was only slightly less fabulous than the hero he would be portraying' and that much of the character's personality was Orson's.

In any case, they had hit on the subject for Welles's movie. Mank was put on a $1,000-a-week contract, forbidden to drink and packed off to Victorville, outside Los Angeles. Welles – apparently at Mank's suggestion – asked Houseman to join Mankiewicz as editor, companion and minder. After 12 weeks Mank delivered a 268-page script, called *American*, composed as an enigmatic prologue followed by a newsreel biography of the subject and then the recollections in flashback of a handful of his acquaintances. Welles loved the challenging structure, witty dialogue and echoing futility but its lead, Charles Foster Kane, was too much like Hearst and the portrait too *journalistic, not very close, the point of view of a newspaperman writing about a newspaper boss he despised.*[86] Orson set about the screenplay with his characteristic editorial rapaciousness, sharpening characters and muddying morality. Scenes and subplots were deleted or distilled to a line or a look; others were altered or added. Did Welles, caught up in the rush, forget that he was cavalierly distorting not a fictional text but the life of one of America's most powerful – and vindictive – men? There were enough changes to specific biographical details to satisfy RKO boss George Schaefer that the parallels with Hearst were deniable, and Kane's personality was by now a far cry from Hearst's. His brashness, his blarney, his rueful self-mockery that never quite reached contrition or humility – that was all Welles, the kind of man who would take on a demigod out of cheek. Yet the man's career – building a newspaper empire on self-important muck-raking, entering politics but failing to achieve his ambitions, constructing a mountain-top fortress stocked with the booty of the world and, most fatefully, the late-blossoming liaison with a young blonde performer – was unmistakably based on Hearst.

By July RKO had approved the script – retitled *Citizen Kane* at Schaefer's suggestion – and a budget of $737,740. Pre-production started. This was where Orson's genius for inspirational leadership came into its own. A film-making novice, he provided something almost unique in Hollywood: an environment in which individual experimentation and technical innovation were encouraged – indeed, demanded. This attracted Gregg Toland, the industry's most accomplished cinematographer, to ask to be Welles's cameraman. An Oscar-winner, he had still struggled to find opportunities to test his most creative ideas but with Welles he developed the flowing continuity of long takes and clever fades so crucial to *Kane*'s momentum, as well as the low angles that provided its ominous monumentality. Wide-angle lenses seemed to stretch cinematic space, already enlarged by 'deep focus' techniques that kept distant objects as sharply defined as those nearby. In the scene where Kane's second wife Susan is discovered after her suicide attempt, for instance, 'deep focus' ensured equal clarity for the pill bottle in the foreground, Susan's bed in the middle distance and the bedroom door in the background; when Kane breaks through the door, the wide-angle photography brings him from tiny, distant figure to looming, overpowering presence in a few short bounds. Such techniques, though not unprecedented, had never been so integral to the shooting of a whole picture and marked a strong contrast with the standard

Hollywood style of cutting between long, medium and close-up shots, with each one expected to supply the viewer with a single, specific perspective or piece of information.

Maurice Seiderman, an enthusiastic amateur from the hairdressing department, created the make-up that would take Kane from 25 to 70, using experimental latex and organic techniques even for scenes of the young Kane. *My whole face was yanked up with pieces of fish-skin in the way old ladies are fixed up nowadays,* Welles later recalled. *I was certainly 25 years old but there's a sort of untouched look about that face you may have noticed, which is impossible in real life.*[87] Intensive planning also went into *Kane*'s sound design. A largely neglected area in movies, its practitioners were among the most eager to demonstrate their ability. Welles, of course, was no novice in the field himself and the film's aural environment is as richly innovative as the more celebrated deep focus. Bernard Herrmann composed his score during shooting so the editing could be designed to fit its movements where required.

Filming started under the guise of test shots while Welles found his feet; for once he avoided the promotional ballyhoo that usually accompanied his new ventures. The shoot generally went well: the movie was essentially composed before filming and each shot already had its designated place in the finished architecture. (If 100 or more takes were needed to get it right, so be it.) The novice cast were familiar with Orson's working practices but innocent of Hollywood convention, while the crew, aware of being involved in something rare and precious, willingly broke with standard studio practice to comply with Welles's insistence on novelty and long working hours.

Orson operated a closed, cloistered set, refusing to allow outsiders to wander in and out of the studio. This bunker mentality may have fostered the *esprit de corps* required to deal with his demanding direction, but the secrecy didn't help Welles's already questionable reputation; to suspend shooting when RKO executives visited was a particularly dubious strategy.

Shooting finished in October, almost on schedule, and Orson embarked on another quick lecture tour in good spirits. Thanks to the extensive preplanning, editing was a formality – apart from the effects and trick work which, though often invisible, formed up to a quarter of the film. By Christmas 1940 the film was more or less done and early reactions were positive. Mank – who had gone to the Screen Writers Guild to ensure he received due credit after read-

Charles Foster Kane, the world at his feet

ing of Welles's casual assertions of authorship – thought the parts he saw 'magnificent'[88] albeit too theatrical and unconventional for popular taste ('too few close-ups' for one thing).

The film was indeed challenging, still is: it begins in a jarring, disorienting fashion, has no heroes or villains and its mystery yields neither solution nor redemption, just a sense of loss and another thing to be burned. *Citizen Kane* offers cold, un-American truths: the unknowability of people, the futility of acquisition. The 'No Trespassing' sign that starts the film as a warning comes by the end to seem a resigned, fatalistic acknowledgement. There is one thing a man can truly possess: his own story, his tragedy, the chip of ice he nurtures in his bosom; yet our pity cannot penetrate the frozen shell around Kane's private sadness.

Kane's glacial splendour

The unreachable figure of Kane was the ideal vehicle for Welles's distanced, larger-than-life performance style: always viewed through another character's perspective, Kane is kept at arm's length from the audience, just as Orson remained wary of the camera's cold, unseduceable eye. *The microphone's a friend, you know. The camera's a critic.*[89] It's no surprise that voice is crucial to *Kane*. The character's first appearance – a shot Welles added during shooting – is a giant close-up of his mouth – like the one planned for the beginning of *Heart of Darkness*, like Coach Roskey's photo. It fills the screen, the maw of a giant in his castle, ready to gobble up the audience, the cinema, the industry. 'Rosebud', it whispers, and the whole film flows from that potent word as the snow globe rolls from his grasp. Later, when young Kane reads his Declaration of Principles – the set of lofty editorial ideals to which he pledges his publishing empire – he leans into the darkness, lest his face give away the emptiness his voice can honey over. The older Kane is mortified when the opera lights go up on him applauding alone (another touch not in the shooting script), as if Orson's radio audience caught him in the act.

Throughout Welles's screen career, there would be a tension between his characters' voices and their presence, a suspicion that the seductive baritone made promises that the exhibition of his body undercut. Time and again Orson worked to effect distance between body and voice: his plans for *Heart of Darkness* had excused him from being photographed (apart from the giant opening close-up of his mouth, which is also the first we see of him in Kane) and he appeared in his next feature, *The Magnificent Ambersons*, only as an unseen narrator. The pattern continued throughout his career: in *The Stranger* his villainous character's most effective speeches are delivered from off-screen, as are many of the soliloquies in Welles's movie of *Macbeth*. There's a scene in *The Lady from Shanghai* in which his character, O'Hara, charms the leading lady through the roof of a horse-drawn buggy, his preposterous blarney about Chinese travels lilting down to her as if by radio or séance. (Could this have been 16-year-old Orson sweet-talking a blushing Connemara girl as his donkey clopped along?) In all these cases Welles used the division of body and voice to promote the power of the voice, letting it weave its magic unobstructed. Later in his career, as we will see, the voice begins to fail.

Gossip, the force that had done so much to shape Welles's career, is crucial to the film too. Time and again we see Kane in the background, framed between two characters discussing him, as if this mythic man were actually conjured from their excited breath. *Citizen Kane* was a story founded on gossip (about both Hearst and Welles), concerned with gossip (which ruins Kane's career and fuels the search for 'Rosebud's' meaning) and the site of gossip, generating more contemporary press coverage than any previous film. That fatal 'Rosebud' blossoms into rumour and innuendo, yet the word evokes a longing to retreat into innocent concealment, to unlive life, to rewind the blown flower into a small, tight bundle of unfulfilled potential. Exposure, Welles's film could have warned him, brings vulnerability.

That was shortly to come. For now, Orson looked on his work and was satisfied. He composed a trailer in which, like the God of Genesis, he appeared as a voice, summoning light, showing off his sound stage and displaying his actors, whom he then prompted into character, having them gossip about Kane on the telephone. He and Houseman, back on terms, discussed a life of Jesus to be made with Toland, and a vehicle for Dolores Del Rio. He also had his people looking into ways to avoid the draft, if it should come to that.

With all this forward planning, did he spare a thought for Hearst? Word was leaking out that this new Welles picture was about the Old Man. Hedda Hopper, one of two gossip columnists who dominated the Hollywood scene, gained entry to a January

1941 preview of *Citizen Kane*. Though she did not work for a Hearst paper, she professed outrage at the 'vicious and irresponsible attack on a great man,'[90] spurring on her rival, Louella Parsons, who did work for Hearst, to see for herself. Parsons demanded a screening and reported back to Hearst, who reportedly responded with the simple cable 'stop citizen kane'. Mention of all RKO pictures was banned from all Hearst papers and Parsons warned the heads of all the major studios that 'Mr Hearst says if you boys want private lives, I'll give you private lives'. Unfounded smears were threatened, along with anti-Semitic accusations about 'foreigners' working in the industry.

Welles offered verbal conjuring tricks in defence of his story, insisting it had been constructed according to *dramaturgical and psychological laws which I recognise to be absolute. They were not colored by the facts in history. The facts in history were actually determined by the same laws which I employed as a dramatist.*[91] He did himself few favours with an article published that February laying into every stratum of the industry. Executives – those with whom his movie's fate rested – were *seriously ignorant . . . absolutely foul . . . high-salaried official[s] with nothing to do but dominate, and no other talent.*[92] MGM's Louis B Mayer offered to refund *Kane*'s production costs if RKO destroyed the negative. The planned 14 February premiere was dropped.

Welles left for New York with Del Rio in tow. Houseman had provided a welcome distraction, inviting him to direct a stage adaptation of *Native Son*, Richard Wright's hit novel illuminating black oppression through the story of a young murderer. Like Kane, Bigger Thomas is an unsympathetic lead boxed in by circumstance and character; like Welles, Wright wanted to avoid trite sentimentality, 'the consolation of tears.'[93] The production was forceful and hyper-cinematic: sound bridges between scenes were vital (a courtroom clock becomes an alarm clock and so on) while chases and shoot-outs staged in and across the auditorium went even further than *Heart of Darkness*'s planned first-person camera in locating the audience within the action. Lights picked out faces isolated in darkness; Welles banned programmes to avoid the distraction, he said, of matches and lighters. *Native Son* opened on 17 March to delighted reviews (the usual concerns about being 'excited rather than moved'[94] notwithstanding) and provided a happy conclusion to the Houseman-Welles partnership.

Meanwhile there was no news on Kane. In martyr mode, Welles cabled Schaefer that *im the only person i know who has any faith in you at all . . . the sympathy and good advice of my friends make their society intolerable . . . my nights are sleepless and my days are a torture*.[95] On 11 March, Schaefer wrote in *Variety* about the importance of free speech. Then Hearst's rival Henry Luce (owner of *Time*, *Life* and *The March of Time*) weighed in on the film's side, as did *Newsweek*. Welles – possibly in concert with Schaefer in a bid to quell internal studio pressure – publicly threatened to sue RKO if the film *wasn't* released. Hearst's papers grew more desperate, attacking the film and Welles as Communist. The anti-*Kane* campaign was looking increasingly ridiculous; Welles successfully sued a gossip columnist who called him a Marxist, noting that *it is not necessarily unpatriotic to disagree with Mr Hearst*. The FBI opened a file on Welles, noting his connections to various leftist groups, but the tide was turning and Schaefer announced premieres in New York, Los Angeles, San Francisco and Chicago for early May.

Welles collapsed with nervous exhaustion and was persuaded to take a couple of weeks' break. His health was not helped by his growing weight: no more inclined to restraint or self-denial in his personal consumption than in his artistic endeavours, Orson now weighed over 15-and-a-half stone (98kg).

The premieres, when they finally came, were damp squibs; there was still a feeling that association with *Kane* might not be good for one's professional health. But the reviews were overwhelmingly sensational, praising in particular the technical innovations. 'Seeing it, it's as if you never really saw a movie before,'[96] said *PM*. Even the *Hollywood Reporter*, one of Orson's chief tormentors in his fallow year after arriving in Hollywood, admitted: 'Mr Genius comes through'. One critic, however, argued that 'the picture is very exciting to anyone who gets excited about how things can be done in the movies [but] what goes on is talk and more talk. And while the stage may stand for this, the movies don't.'[97] Others began to wonder what was at the bottom of this bag of tricks. And despite a massive publicity push – 'SEE WHY AMERICA IS ONE BIG GOSSIP COLUMN ABOUT ORSON WELLES/CITIZEN KANE!'[98] – ticket sales were modest. Pressure from Hearst's organisation certainly restricted the film's distribution, but even where it was shown it seldom made a profit. As one North Dakota cinema manager succinctly put it, 'It may be a classic, but it's plum "nuts" to your show-going public.'[99] Nominated for nine awards at the 1942 Oscars, its single win was for the screenplay, the area where, thanks to Mankiewicz's insistence on Screen Writers' Guild arbitration, Welles's contribution was most obviously in question.

It is unknown whether William Randolph Hearst ever actually saw *Citizen Kane*, though Welles told the story of how he bumped into the Old Man in a lift before the San Francisco opening and offered him seats. *He didn't answer and I got off the elevator thinking, as I still do, that if he had been Charles Foster Kane he would have taken the tickets and gone.*[100]

Only God and Orson know 1941–42

'The things that we have and that we think are so solid . . .
they're like smoke. [It] seems all thick and black and busy
against the sky, as if it were going to do such important things
and last forever, and you see it getting thinner and thinner –
and then, in a little while, it isn't there at all.'

Booth Tarkington, *The Magnificent Ambersons*[101]

Citizen Kane's poor performance at the box office was perhaps Orson's first real failure; to have created so masterful a fireworks display yet not win the love of the people must have been disconcerting. But if, that summer of 1941, 26-year-old Welles was entertaining doubts, they barely showed – although perhaps his professional debut as a magician, dismembering Dolores Del Rio at a state fair, was a form of consolation.

The search was already on for his second movie project: he toyed with *Cyrano de Bergerac* (the ultimate false-nose role) and an idea based on the French murderer Landru (eventually sold to Chaplin, who made it as *Monsieur Verdoux*). *The Way to Santiago*, a Nazis-in-Mexico melodrama that concluded with a rousing radio broadcast, was deemed too politically sensitive and Welles and Cotten began adapting another globetrotting thriller, *Journey Into Fear*. Orson's interest in South America also extended to *It's All True*, an ambitious if vague idea for a portmanteau documentary. For one of its stories – 'My Friend Bonito', about a boy and his bull – Orson scouted Mexican locations and charged Mercury's

Norman Foster with gathering footage. There was a new radio show too, featuring stories, music, comedy and commentary, plus such guest performers as Del Rio, Lucille Ball, Ginger Rogers and rising star Rita Hayworth.

Welles had now decided on his follow-up to *Citizen Kane*: a film based on Booth Tarkington's novel *The Magnificent Ambersons*, about a proud, aristocratic Midwestern family's decline. There were personal parallels for Orson in the story of a doting, dying mother, Isabel, her spoiled son, George, who gets his comeuppance, and automobile inventor Eugene Morgan, whom Orson boldly claimed Tarkington had modelled on his father Dick. The tale's romantic crisis – George's pride and vanity prevent old flames Isabel and Eugene from rekindling their youthful love – is mirrored by the family's material ruin as the motor age overtakes their dynastic complacency. Like *Kane*, *Ambersons* has no sympathetic lead and offers no consolation in its picture of unforgiving, all-devouring time; the plot engines are gossip, reputation and nostalgia.

Too big and worldly to convince as such a petty person as George, Welles surprisingly but brilliantly cast cowboy actor Tim Holt. Cotten was Eugene, Anne Baxter his daughter Lucy, Ray Collins played Uncle Jack and Agnes Moorehead – so disconcerting in her cameo as Kane's mother – got the role of her career as neurotic Aunt Fanny. Silent screen veterans Dolores Costello and Richard Bennett were cast as Isabel and her father, the patriarch Major Amberson. Welles would narrate.

RKO's George Schaefer approved a budget substantially above the studio's official limit and preparations went ahead with characteristic gusto – and the aid of the Mercury's new manager Jack Moss, a hulking former professional magician. Welles planned long, unbroken takes, a stately classicism to succeed *Kane*'s baroque flourishes. A month's rehearsals led to the idea of pre-recording the dialogue and having the actors mime to it, eliminating the problem of camera noises. This plan to have the cast possessed by voices from above proved maddeningly distracting and was dropped on the first morning of filming, 28 October 1941. Shooting went smoothly, as long as Welles's perfectionism was satisfied: insisting on condensed breath and real snow for the winter excursion scene, Orson filmed in an icehouse, sitting wrapped up with brandy as he asked Holt and Baxter to roll down that drift one more time. The place stank of fish, made the lights explode and gave Collins pneumonia but yielded a scene that could have been filmed in *Kane*'s snow globe. The long takes of the ball sequence took 90 hours and 100 technicians.

Orson was also pleased with Norman Foster's Mexican footage for 'My Friend Bonito', achieved despite bad weather, illness, deaths by train and bull and the constant threat of bandits. *It's All True* now received backing from the Office of Inter-American Affairs, which had been set up to improve relations between the US and its southern neighbours, considered vulnerable to fascism. Its co-ordinator Nelson Rockefeller was a major RKO stockholder and a film was considered a good way to promote goodwill. When the Japanese attacked Pearl Harbor on 7 December, Welles made a stirring radio broadcast and began preparing to go to Brazil to shoot the Carnival. (He was by now confirmed unfit for service with 'chronic myoditis and original syndrome arthritis, bronchial asthma, high fever and inverted flat feet.'[102])

He cracked on with *Ambersons* and put *Journey Into Fear* into production as well, recalling Foster to direct it (thereby condemning 'Bonito' to limbo). The story of an innocent American (Cotten) adrift on a sea of international intrigue, *Journey* was subject to constant script changes imposed to avoid implications of 'immorality' or causing offence to the half dozen nations from which its villains came. There were also changes to the cast, which included Moorehead and Del Rio. Mercury manager Jack Moss played a bizarrely conspicuous but disquietingly mute assassin and Richard Bennett's ship's captain was a kind of parody of

Major Amberson. As secret police chief Colonel Haki, all bold nose and bushy moustache, Welles got to swill brandy, smoke cigars, speak French with a Turkish accent and flirt with the lead's wife. These outlandish performances are the film's main pleasure; the hobbled script makes it hard to engage with as a suspense thriller.

Working on *Ambersons* during the day and *Journey Into Fear* at night, Welles completed shooting on the former by 31 January 1942, and finished his scenes in the latter a couple of days later. With RKO approval for four months' location work in Brazil, Orson made his excuses to his radio audience, put together a very rough cut of *Ambersons* with Robert Wise (his editor on *Kane*) and headed to Rio de Janeiro in full expectation of continuing editing from there. He was equally blasé about his next film: at the airport he told a reporter *I've got no script, no actors, no preconceived ideas. I'm going down there with a camera, and I hope to record something that will be of interest to the people of all the Americas.*[103] So he headed off to one of the dark places of the earth, forsaking a project he shouldn't have let out of his sight for one that was barely a twinkle in his eye.

Years later he told his biographer Barbara Leaming he spent the fiesta *all covered with confetti, trying to pretend I like carnivals, you know. I hate carnivals.*[104] Those who saw him learning to samba (a dance was named after him), cruising around town in his police-escorted convertible (to shouts of 'Orson is coming! Orson is coming!'), or working his way through the feisty local girls ('quickies by the thousands!' his secretary recalled), might have had other ideas.

In order to compete with other travelogues, RKO had ordered *It's All True* to be shot in Technicolor, so Welles had arrived in Rio with a day or two to prepare filming one of the world's largest, least controllable festivals with one of the industry's most complex technologies. Without the supportive collaboration of his Mercury cronies, Orson was arguably more alone than at any

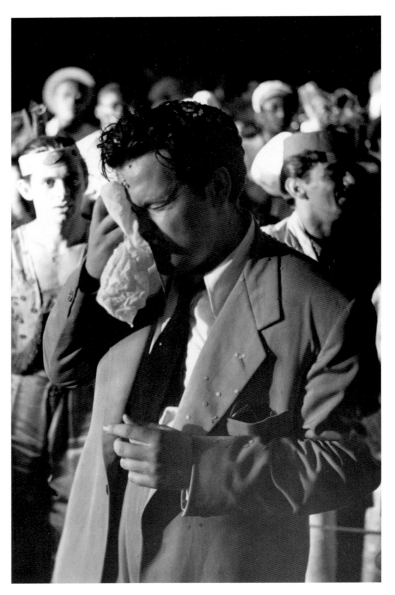

Welles covered in confetti

time since his trip to Morocco. He spent his time editing *Ambersons*, leaving his carnival crew to fend for themselves. Orson had also heard about the *jangadeiros*, impoverished fishermen from Fortaleza who had sailed 1,600 miles down the coast to protest about their living conditions. Their leader, Jacaré, was something of a national treasure, small and wiry, with dancing eyes. Welles thought the story marvellous; but wouldn't it be even better if they arrived just in time for Carnival? To restage this 'live' event (it's all true, of course) Welles left a near-mutinous crew on 5 March to fetch the four men down to Rio from Fortaleza. The rest of the month was spent planning recreations of Carnival, sheltering from the rain with a succession of local girls and not returning calls from Dolores Del Rio, whose hints at marriage Orson had finessed away before his departure. Soon after she publicly terminated their affair.

Welles's interest in Rio's street-level nightlife and *favelas* (shanty-towns) alarmed the Brazilian authorities while, back in Hollywood, certain RKO executives were dismissing the Rio footage as 'a lot of jigaboos jumping up and down'[105]. Growing unease at *Ambersons'* sombre tone and internal political upheavals at the studio further weakened Schaefer and Welles's position. The latest cut of *Ambersons* didn't reach Welles until 15 March, by which time RKO's new head of production was demanding that its 132-minute running time be reduced. A preview screening two days later at Pomona, California provided further justification, with most of the audience confirming Tarkington's own prediction that his readers might be 'not only scornfully amused but vaguely angered'[106] by the tale. (At the same time, other viewers thought it 'the best cinema has yet offered.'[107]) Schaefer was badly shaken and Wise, Moss and even Cotten wrote to Orson expressing concerns at the film's poor reception and suggesting he return to defend his work. Instead he sent more insistent memos and demanded more funds.

Shooting in Rio was troubled: recreations of fights, samba schools and the background to the *jangadeiros'* arrival had not gone to plan, but Welles refused to placate the studio. An RKO publicist reported that 'he has a cane bottomed rocking chair which is liable to turn over at any moment, loose bowels and the disposition of a teething baby – that's in the mornings. After a lunch of spaghetti, black beans and fresh cheese his humor improves and he's pretty good company. By nightfall he's ready for the Urca Casino. After midnight he likes to write. Anyhow, that's his story . . . As for the film story, only God and Orson know; and Orson doesn't remember.'[108] Others on the crew fuelled RKO's concerns – in tune with the racist prejudices of the day – that an interest in the country's street life was at best tasteless, at worst immoral. An RKO suggestion to remove scenes in which 'mulattoes or *mestizos* appear too conspicuously' makes one wonder what they expected footage of Brazilians to show.

A full month into the dispute over *Ambersons*, on 15 April, Welles cabled Moss demanding no cuts be made. Yet in Hollywood the studio had already excised a third of the running time, mostly from the downbeat second half of the picture, and was preparing reshoots of certain scenes to soften the tone. The concluding encounter between Eugene and Fanny – which Welles had darkened from the book, setting it in a shabby, gossip-infested boarding house – was reimagined in saccharine, sentimental soft-focus. The studio's cut substantially mitigated the harshness of Welles's vision and made the Ambersons' decline – so delicately balanced against their glory in Welles's original screenplay – seem jarringly sudden, even simplistic. Yet it remains an Orson Welles picture. His narration – the first 15 seconds of which are intoned over a black screen – was unusually subjective, even interacting with the town gossips who form the story's chorus, and extended to his reading the credits rather than printing them. In its truncated form, *The Magnificent Ambersons*

Agnes Moorehead and Tim Holt in *The Magnificent Ambersons*

isn't the masterpiece it promises to be. Instead, in keeping with the story's preoccupation with lost opportunities, it became the first of many projects of which Orson could wistfully say 'if you'd only seen it as I intended . . . ' *I was absolutely certain of its value,* he would later insist, *much more than of Kane.*[109]

Back in Brazil, over $100,000 was spent on shooting *It's All True* in March and April alone; Schaefer cabled Orson complaining that he had 'no realization of money spent or problems of recouping costs.'[110] In response, Welles asked for another $150,000 to recreate a dance sequence. By 18 May Schaefer was offering $30,000 for an immediate wrap-up. The following day – as the final *Ambersons* retakes were being shot in Hollywood – Jacaré drowned while shooting the *jangadeiros'* arrival in Rio. Orson shared the Brazilians' grief and on 13 June took a crew up to Fortaleza and shot lyrical, touching, impressionistic sequences about a young fisherman's marriage, death and funeral. He was there for a month, during which time RKO cut him loose. Welles's lack of fiscal or creative accountability was no doubt partly to blame, but the conclusive factor in RKO's decision may have been, as some critics have argued, Orson's 'radical pro-black stance, including the fact that he enjoyed the company and collaboration of blacks, as well as his insistence on featuring non-whites as the pivotal characters in both the film's Brazilian episodes.'[111]

On 1 July the Mercury team was told to vacate the RKO lot; on 10 July *Ambersons* was released without fanfare. The *New York Times* thought it 'distinctly not attuned to the times . . . With a world inflamed, nations shattered, populations in rags, with massacres and bombings, Welles devotes 9,000 feet of film to a spoiled brat who grows up as a spoiled, spiteful young man.'[112] By the end of the month Schaefer was out too and Orson had returned to Rio to find full-page ads in which RKO disavowed responsibility for his actions or debts; the Office of Inter-American Affairs and US Embassy also rejected him. The $1.2 million-worth of

It's All True footage was all but written off. Welles was contractually permitted to tinker with *Journey Into Fear* while trying to cobble together a supporting feature out of his South American adventure, but RKO's express aim was 'to get rid of this property and Orson Welles if there is any way to do it.'[113] Despite repeated efforts over the coming years, Orson never would produce a viable cut.

Since arriving in New York aged 19, Welles had been granted the resources of a major network, a Hollywood studio and two government departments to pursue his artistic ambitions. Now he returned home with nothing but his reputation – which wasn't what it used to be. Partly to justify its failure to recoup its investment in Welles, RKO had cultivated an image of wanton profligacy that would prove as potent as Orson's boy wonder persona. He was only 27 years old, but his career would never recover: the prodigy who had electrified Broadway, scandalised the airwaves and reimagined the moving picture was out in the cold.

The best kind of showmanship 1942–45

'I am the best, I know that, now what do I do with it?'
Senator Blake Pellarin, *The Big Brass Ring*[114]

Throughout his young life, Orson had rarely struggled to find backers for projects about which he was passionate, largely thanks to his reputation for artistic boldness and popular accessibility. That changed forever with the horrified response to *The Magnificent Ambersons* and *It's All True*: if this is how a genius gets things done, the studios thought, we'll do without. But he remained a globally famous performer and proceeded to capitalise on his fame, embracing professional celebrity in a way he had never had to before. He became a fixture at the parties he had avoided and a regular guest star on radio, correcting the host on quiz shows or sending himself up on Jack Benny. He also had radio series of his own, on South American history and the aviation industry – part of the war effort and strongly anti-fascist and progressive-liberal in tone. A young Arthur Miller, charged with finding a format for the aviation show, concluded 'your voice is a format' in its own right. Miller was amazed by Welles's microphone technique: 'he seemed to climb into it, his word-carving voice winding into one's brain. No actor had such intimacy and sheer presence in a loudspeaker.'[115]

While publicly lamenting Hollywood's aversion to experiment, Orson cultivated his career as a leading man. In December 1942 David Selznick offered him Mr Rochester in *Jane Eyre*, a role that allowed him to brood and glower and be paid $100,000 for doing so. Welles also contributed to the script. On the back of the film's success he accepted the lead in *Tomorrow is Forever* (a silly variation on the Martin Guerre story). Acting, along with radio, was to become Orson's day job, a somewhat tedious means of earning cash; though he never failed to deliver a performance (or something that smelled like one), working for others didn't come naturally to him. Sometimes he threw tantrums. Sometimes he was on his best behaviour. Sometimes he tried to make things fun, playing pranks on the girls or letting the director in on how he could make a better picture.

Despite his substantial debts and child support obligations, almost half of Orson's *Jane Eyre* wages went on the *Mercury Wonder Show*, a sawdust-and-peanuts circus act mounted in a big top on Cahuenga Boulevard with clowns, cats and acrobats. Conceived as entertainment for the troops, it was also an excuse for 'The Great Orson' to eat fire, catch bullets and mesmerise chickens, and ran to packed audiences throughout August 1943.

One trick the public never got to see was Orson's cutting Rita Hayworth in half. The pair had struck up an unlikely romance after working together on radio; Welles had pursued the actress, who had recently become a major star and was now the forces' sweetheart. 'Beauty and the Brain', the gossip columns called them, but he provided sympathetic, constructive attention of a kind she had rarely known, while he got to bask in her glorious receptivity. Rita was a keen volunteer for the *Wonder Show*

Rita and Orson in the *Wonder Show*

Rita Hayworth (1918–1987) was born Marguerite Cansino in Brooklyn, the daughter of dancers. She danced professionally from the age of 12 and appeared in her first movie aged 17. Businessman Edward Judson, whom she married in 1937, dyed her hair red, changed her name and got her contracted to Columbia Pictures. *Only Angels Have Wings* (1939) was her breakthrough role, leading to films with Fred Astaire and Gene Kelly. Her picture was on the atomic warhead dropped on the Bikini atoll. *Gilda* (1946) marked the pinnacle of her career. She married four times and continued to act into the 1970s.

but her boss at Columbia, Harry Cohn, was having none of it. (Among her replacements was Orson's pal Marlene Dietrich.) However, in a break from shooting wedding scenes for *Cover Girl* on 7 September, Hayworth became the second Mrs Orson Welles. 'The morning after we were married,' she later reported, 'I woke up and I could tell by the expression on his face, he was just waiting for the applause.'[116]

Orson struggled to find a directorial project, but his attention seems already to have been leaning towards politics. That year he had given speeches on education and racism and wrote the introduction for a pamphlet about the victimisation of Mexican American youths in a notorious police scandal. It was Louis Dolivet – a well-funded, well-connected French Partisan refugee and founder of the internationalist Free World organisation – who persuaded Welles that a political career was a real possibility. On meeting through mutual friends, Barbara Leaming writes, he found Welles 'relatively unsophisticated in the complexities of world affairs, [but] saw that the showman possessed what he took for the "right instincts" with regard to political issues.'[117] Dolivet – the last mentor figure attracted to Welles, the last to see untapped potential – soon had him writing editorials for the *Free World* magazine (on racial hatred, anti-fascism and, later, the atom bomb) and speaking at public meetings alongside senior British, Chinese and Spanish ministers. *Oh, he had great plans! He was going to organise it so that in 15 years I was going to get the Nobel Prize.*[118] Orson's contributions were perhaps more electrifying than substantial; politics for Welles was performance. Once, after rousingly delivering a speech written by Dolivet, he was humiliated when unable to field questions; his ignorance of fine detail was, he admitted, *problematical.*[119]

Not that Orson's engagement with the issues was insincere or faddish; he was among the first to warn that the *phony fear of Communism is smoke-screening the real menace of renascent Fascism*[121] and he irked the sponsors of his new radio show – a collection of skits, songs, readings and topical commentary called *Orson Welles's Almanac* – by treating black guests such as Duke Ellington as respected equals. In May 1944 Welles became a nominal employee of the Department of the Treasury, co-ordinating the Fifth War Loan Drive, a mammoth, starry radio broadcast that attracted an enormous audience. And that September he hit the trail for Roosevelt's fourth election campaign. Spending $10,000 of his own money, he spoke all over the country and became one of the President's most prominent advocates: he even stood in for FDR in a nationally transmitted debate with his opponent Thomas Dewey, and delivered the Democrats' pre-election radio broadcast. He exchanged telegrams with Roosevelt during and after the campaign; following victory FDR thanked him for his role 'in the unrehearsed reality of the drama of the American future. It was a great show, in which you played a great part.'[122] Shortly after the war, Orson insisted he had given serious consideration to running for the Senate in his home state of Wisconsin in 1944. *My opponent would have been Joe McCarthy*, he later mused, *so I've got him on my conscience.*[123]

That December, Rita gave birth to Rebecca – in whom, Orson's secretary reported, he was 'not really all that interested. I don't think he ever paid any attention to her.'[124] He had another radio series, a return to literary adaptations called *This Is My Best*, and in early 1945 tried to sell a series of political commentaries. His knowing argument that there was *real showmanship – the best kind of showmanship – in Orson Welles doing a big national column*[125] did not prove persuasive. The *New York Post* – for whom he had written occasional guest columns – did however offer Orson a regular slot, for which he assiduously mugged up, even if the supposedly daily feature rarely appeared more than two or three times a week. *I don't have the answers to the world's problems*, he conceded to his inaugural readers, *but I do believe that if I can stir the people to debate and think about our problems, we'll find a way out*.[126] Initially a ragbag of memoir, politics, showbiz and top tips, the column grew increasingly militant, especially after Roosevelt's death in April. Welles's strident anti-fascism – not to mention his talk of *America's complacent moral superiority*[127] – was not a hit with readers. He was dispirited to be asked by the *Post*'s editors to concentrate on showbiz.

There was further disillusionment when *This Is My Best* was axed. The final straw had been his last minute attempt to replace the scheduled show with *The Taming of the Shrew* starring him and Rita – a choice that, consciously or not, reflected their growing marital friction. Asked how she coped with his personality, Hayworth once replied: 'He goes his way and I go with him.'[128] Although their marriage seems initially to have been idyllic, the combination of Rita's insecurities and Orson's aversion to domesticity proved unworkable, though the pair remained fond of each other.

Orson and Rita with Rebecca (far left) and Christopher

The prospect of his securing political office became increasingly remote and, though he would remain engaged in social activism, Welles's attention reverted to Hollywood. In early 1945, Sam Spiegel of the fledgling International Pictures offered him the lead in *The Stranger*, about a Nazi living as a Connecticut schoolteacher, and Welles wangled the directing gig too – albeit under an indemnity clause because of his now-dubious reputation. It was the first and only movie he directed as a job of work: *I wanted to do a film to prove to the industry that I could direct a standard Hollywood picture, on time and on budget, just like anyone else.*[129] Committed to a conventional, audience-friendly approach, and keen to look the part for another attractively menacing leading role, Welles underwent daily weight loss injections in his buttocks.

Filmed over June and July of 1945, *The Stranger* came in early, under budget and without the dynamism and character that distinguish Welles's other films. The studio cut as irrelevant the opening scenes, set in South America; these, Welles insisted, were by far the film's finest sequences. Even so, there is plenty to enjoy in *The Stranger*: the rich sound design offers multi-layered conversations at the drug store and tea parties of gossip-suffused Harper – a town Welles consciously based on Woodstock, just as the school in the film was modelled on Todd. Welles post-dubbed several characters himself, as he would in many later projects too. Like *Journey Into Fear, The Stranger* uses tongue-in-cheek humour to offset its melodrama – Kindler idly doodles a swastika while on the telephone – yet remarkably its newsreel scene also gave many of its viewers their first view of the reality of the concentration camps. Welles's central performance, however, is distanced, almost distracted. Kindler doesn't unleash that knowing, threatening smirk until the climax, when he looks down from his bell-tower eyrie at the dots below, as superior and doomed as Harry Lime on his wheel in *The Third Man*. Following his own experiences of failure, the punishment of hubris – always a fascination of Welles's – was now hardwired into his vision.

A bright cruel world and night's black agents 1945–47

The Stranger had demonstrated Orson's ability to deliver within the system, but the dispiriting experience convinced him *that I'd rather do what I didn't like very much as an actor than what I didn't like very much as a director.*[130] It had rekindled his love of cinema, however: he wrote in the *New York Times* that *we should have theatres financed by the Government for private film experimentation.*[131] He continued with his political activity as well: he revived his *New York Post* column, on hold while he was making *The Stranger*, and he started a year-long radio series of social and political commentaries.

After spending Christmas 1945 alone on a Mexican pyramid Orson embarked on a project that would combine past triumphs with the ultimate in globe-trotting escapism: a Broadway production of Jules Verne's *Around the World in 80 Days*, which Welles had performed on radio and proposed as a film to Schaefer. It would be a grand extravaganza, a carnivalesque spectacle encompassing theatre, dance, film, circus and song. New York producer Mike Todd provided backing and also the possibility of another, strikingly different collaboration: the English language premier of Brecht's *Life of Galileo*, to be staged with Charles Laughton after *Around the World in 80 Days*.

Orson and Rita's separation, finalised during *The Stranger*'s shoot, was publicly acknowledged when he decamped east. The show left no time for brooding: there were three dozen scenes, 200 costumes, a Japanese circus, Hindu temple (with elephant) and moving train (with collapsing bridge) to coordinate. Cole Porter would provide the songs, Orson would conjure as the Great Foo San and film silent slapstick inserts like those planned for *Too Much Johnson*. Welles continued to conceive new ideas rather than rehearsing and perfecting those already commissioned, or addressing the script and songs' shortcomings. As the costs spiralled Orson secured additional funds from Porter, film industry associates and even his driver, 'Shorty' Chirello. Not long before opening, the costumes were held back because of unpaid storage costs. Desperate, Orson called Harry Cohn, offering his services as a director to Columbia in exchange for bailing him out. As Orson told it, he proposed an adaptation of Sherwood King's pulpy *If I Die Before I Wake* on the strength of a glimpse of a nearby paperback copy; in fact, Columbia had already optioned the novel.

When Orson announced, 10 days before opening, that he intended to strike oil on stage every night, Todd quit in despair. Once more, Welles professed astonishment that a sponsor should find anything questionable in his behaviour. The pre-Broadway tryout run began on 27 April in Boston: cues were missed, stagehands visible, props unreliable. 'Is this London?' one character asked. 'Yes,' came the reply as a backdrop of the Rockies heaved into view. 'This is London, all right.' More than once Welles opened the show with an apology. The practical problems were largely ironed out in time for the New York opening on 31 May, which coincided with a new run of the *Mercury Summer Theatre on the Air* (beginning with a promotional adaptation of *80 Days*). Some critics found the play bold and invigorating, others pointlessly expansive; when the *World-Telegram* noted the absence of the kitchen sink, Welles wheeled one on that night as an encore. Like *Horse Eats Hat*, it developed a core of dedicated fans. It did not, however, make money. By the end of its two-month run Welles had accrued debts of $320,000 – the basis of the IRS tax burden that would dog him for the rest of his life.

Meanwhile Welles had neglected *Galileo*. He couldn't countenance working with Todd after the producer had (Orson felt) betrayed him by walking out on *80 Days*, and greeted Laughton's attempts to patch up the rift with petulant resentment. In a letter of 25 July Laughton told Welles 'you are an extraordinary man of the theatre, and therefore I flatly do not believe that you cannot function as a member of a team'[132] — which showed appreciation for Welles's talent rather than familiarity with his methods. 'Todd has never spoken ill of you to either of us,' Laughton pleaded on his and Brecht's behalf. 'The strongest word he had used is 'afraid'.'[133] After further failed attempts at mollification, Welles was let go.

Orson still maintained an active interest in politics and public speaking but in July the sponsors of his radio commentaries withdrew their support from the low-rated series. The network, ABC, agreed to keep it on air for a nominal wage while a new sponsor was sought. (Orson had previously netted $1,700 a week.) Later that month the National Association for the Advancement of Colored People (NAACP) sent Welles an affidavit in which Isaac Woodward, Jr, a decorated black veteran, testified to having been beaten blind by South Carolina police officers. Reading it out on air, Welles started the most effective political action of his life, a perfect blend of righteous rhetoric and melodramatic showmanship pegged to a single, concrete issue. *Wash your hands, Officer X*, he commanded the unnamed culprit. *Wash them well. Scrub and scour . . . We will blast out your name. We'll give the world your given name, Officer X. Yes, and your so-called Christian name . . . Officer X, after I have found you out, I'll never lose you. If they try you, I'm going to watch the trial. If they jail you, I'm going to wait for your first day of freedom. You won't be free of me . . . Who am I? A masked avenger from the comic books? No, sir. Merely an inquisitive citizen of America.*[134] The combination of vaudeville and classical tropes is pure Welles — the Shadow haunts Macbeth. Over the next month he repeatedly returned to the affair, lending it the narrative appeal of a crime serial while stoking national concern at the injustice of the case. For added immediacy he read NAACP bulletins hot off the press, infuriating ABC. By September charges had been brought and the officer responsible sentenced to a year's imprisonment. Welles did not go to watch the trial, but he did petition (unsuccessfully) for a higher sentence. The NAACP singled Orson out as largely responsible for the conviction; the radio series was dropped a month later.

That July had also seen the release of *The Stranger*, which achieved its aim insofar as it turned a profit – the only film Welles ever directed to do so on initial release. In a field where one's last effort tends to eclipse its predecessors, the architect of the ruinous *Kane*, ruined *Ambersons* and rumour-plagued *It's All True* was now considered potentially bankable. Extensive discussions with the British producer Alexander Korda began, and Welles had *If I Die Before I Wake* to make for Harry Cohn, as writer, producer, director and star (but without final cut). Over a weekend he adapted the novel into *The Lady from Shanghai*, dressing its noirish plot with exotic locations, twisted characterisations and baroque, dreamlike stylisation. Rather than the übermensch he usually embodied, Welles would play a naïve Irish sailor, Mike O'Hara, who is ensnared in a complex set-up by the beautiful Elsa Bannister, her crippled lawyer husband Arthur and his outré partner Grisby. Orson had a European actress in mind for Elsa but Cohn had a surprising suggestion: Rita Hayworth was keen to play the part. Still on good terms with Orson, she may have been hoping to rekindle their marriage (or get better support for Rebecca), or she may have been thinking professionally: she could benefit from him stretching her artistically. Orson, meanwhile, could benefit from Rita's reflected glamour: her attachment pushed *The Lady from Shanghai*'s budget up to $2.3 million – which meant keener interest from Cohn, who had reservations about America's sweetheart having her famous red hair dyed blonde for the part, let alone being cast as a double-crossing murderer.

Location work began in Acapulco in October, on board Errol Flynn's yacht. Flynn didn't appear in the film but, despite the political chasm between them, he and Welles got on famously. (Flynn introduced Orson to cocaine, which, in a rare show of self-restraint, he realised he could not afford to become accustomed to.) During shooting the alcoholic Flynn kvetched over the state of the ship, beat up a bartender for being 'a filthy kike'[135] and, the second his pregnant wife departed, took off with a statuesque local beauty, delaying work for several days. There were other problems: on the first take the assistant director keeled over with a fatal heart attack (Flynn was all for stitching him in a duffel bag and burying him at sea); the glare from the sun was too harsh during the day while insects blocked the lights at night; Rita was sick and Orson badly bitten on the eye; spear-fishers were required for the swimming scenes to guard against barracuda. But the footage was terrific. Shooting continued in San Francisco, though Hayworth's illness caused four weeks' delay, contributing to the production eventually running $416,000 over budget.

By the end of March, Orson had delivered a two-and-a-half-hour cut. When Cohn saw it he reportedly offered $1,000 for an explanation of the plot. Demanding more close-ups, a new ending and an explicatory voice-over, he had an hour chopped out (which didn't aid clarity) and imposed an editor to rationalise the picture's style. Orson struggled to retain the outlandishness that was to him the film's point. He told Cohn he wanted to give it *something off-center, queer, strange . . . a bad dream aspect . . . a quality of freshness and strangeness*[136] to distinguish it from a common or garden whodunit – which was precisely what Cohn was after. A long tracking shot from the opening sequence was lost, as was much of the climactic shoot-out in a fairground, which Orson had laboriously designed and even painted himself. (The remaining

The treachery of images: *The Lady from Shanghai*'s hall of mirrors

shoot-out in the fairground's maze of mirrors, however, became one of Welles's trademark scenes.) Most damaging was the effect on the soundtrack. Echoing footsteps, a wind-and-water background Orson had sweated over in Acapulco, concatenations of Mexican and American voices, a complex layered design accompanying O'Hara's flight from the staged shooting – all disappeared. The score was reworked around a song Cohn insisted Elsa sing and embellished with twee, illustrative flourishes. Cohn still wasn't satisfied and delayed release. When the film did come out with minimal publicity in May 1948, the reviews echoed O'Hara's verdict on the affair: *all very rich and rare and strange, but I had had no stomach for it.*

It is an odd picture, hard to follow in its surviving cut and of distinctly curdled humour. Again Welles offered no really sympathetic characters: Elsa, Bannister and Grisby are snakes writhing in a bag – or, in the film's memorable analogy, frenzied sharks feeding off one another – and O'Hara is a puzzle, so knowing about his naiveté that you wonder what he's up to. A sickly, sweaty evil suffuses the cruise from New York to San Francisco – surely the weirdest version of that city ever put on screen, with its aquarium of monstrously magnified fish and courtroom that collapses into vaudeville (not the last time Welles would present the judicial system as a form of comic theatre). To watch *The Lady from Shanghai* is to surrender to a trip every bit as queasy and disorientating as O'Hara's time on that yacht – hardly ideal Saturday night fare for a post-war America preparing to boom. *Friends avoided me*, Welles remembered. *Whenever it was mentioned, people would clear their throats and change the subject . . . I only found out it was considered a good picture when I got to Europe.*[137]

Welles's next project would be equally deformed and unpalatable, replacing *The Lady from Shanghai*'s 'bright, cruel world' with the exploits of 'night's black agents'. It was prompted by an invitation from the Edinburgh Festival to mount a play: Welles thought *Macbeth* an apt choice and wondered if the production could double as preparation for a quickie film to be shot straight afterwards. The Edinburgh production fell through but the idea survived: the Utah Centennial Festival mounted the play and Republic Pictures, home of disposable cowboy-and-Indian quickies, stumped up $884,000 for a bit of prestige. The text was reconfigured, framing Macbeth's murderous ascendancy within a battle between the witches' ancient, amorphous chaos and the rigid new Christian faith, with its geometric Celtic crosses. It was a savage world, more Tartar than tartan, cursed with a damned warlord for a king. This was not a lavish 'show, show,

A poor player

show' like the voodoo spectacular mounted on Broadway a decade earlier. Now Welles told the story of a gifted man of whom absolute greatness is mischievously prophesied, only for him to damn himself in its achievement.

The brief run, 28 to 31 May 1947, delighted Salt Lake City and preparations went ahead for the soundstage shoot. Welles was demanding, economical and imaginative: he would perform in one scene while directing another across the studio; he put cameramen in costume and sent them into battle scenes to get handheld footage. The set's blatant artificiality – the papier-mâché lunar crags, the thorny castle that seems more cage than keep, the caves trickling with water or blood – worked towards a claustrophobic, dreamlike unity that perhaps belongs less to cinema than theatre or radio. The presentation of the soliloquies muddies the gap between physical and mental space, with dislocated voices whispering dreamily over almost-abstract shots of mist and moors. In more active scenes the performances are allowed to unfold theatrically in extremely long takes. Jeanette Nolan, a radio colleague of Welles's, was a no-nonsense Lady Macbeth (Agnes Moorehead was unavailable), Roddy McDowall played Malcolm and many small parts went to friends or family: Orson's driver Shorty Chirello played the Macbeths' factotum and Christopher Welles was cast as Macduff's son. Welles's decaying, dissolute Macbeth is an actor king, never more alive than when spinning his yarn about Duncan's death, never more self-aware than in his realisation that 'Life's but a walking shadow, a poor player / That struts and frets his hour upon the stage / And then is heard no more.'

Completed in a remarkable 23 days – and under budget too – *Macbeth* was hailed by Republic's boss Herbert Yates as 'the greatest individual job of acting, directing, adapting and producing that to my knowledge Hollywood has ever seen.'[138] The dubbing, scoring and editing did not seem to present significant challenges and so Welles left them under the supervision of his assistant Richard Wilson and set off for London, to meet with the producer Alexander Korda. That decision was to prove almost as damaging to his work and reputation as the decision to desert the editing of *The Magnificent Ambersons* for Rio de Janeiro had been five years earlier.

Masters of suggestion 1947–50

'He just made everything seem like such fun.
He could fix anything . . . '

Holly Martins on Harry Lime in *The Third Man*

The dreadful precedent of *Ambersons* notwithstanding, Welles's confidence wasn't without justification. *The Stranger* had turned a profit, he had a Rita Hayworth picture awaiting release and the *Macbeth* shoot had been a model of efficiency. With Korda at London Films he discussed films of *Around the World in 80 Days, Cyrano de Bergerac, Salomé, Carmen, Moby Dick* and *Othello*. Another producer, Edward Small, offered him the role of the shyster magician Cagliostro in *Black Magic*, shooting in Rome. Welles installed himself at the Excelsior hotel and, he reported, lectured cardinals on Catholicism, filled Pius XII in on the latest Hollywood gossip, attended orgies and avoided 'Lucky' Luciano, who wanted Orson to make his life story. The few dollars he had went further in post-war Europe, he found, and he had admirers there. Back home, the House Committee on un-American Activities was beginning its work – though, despite his FBI file, Welles never seems to have been a particular target. No, the federal body he needed to avoid was the IRS.

On set, he threw his weight around and acted as if Cagliostro's powers of suggestion were his own. Nights were spent working on the editing of *Macbeth*; Republic were now uncomfortable with the porridgey Scottish accents Welles had his cast use, and there were other soundtrack problems. Republic cut more than

20 minutes and pushed back the December 1947 release date; well into the next year the editors were waiting 'for records of Orson breathing'[139] to arrive from Rome. Intended to show that Welles could work quickly and efficiently, *Macbeth* began to suggest the opposite, a reputation not helped by its last-minute withdrawal from the Venice Film Festival in September 1948. When it was finally seen *Il Tempo* thought it gave Shakespeare 'a new and magic dimension, abstract and miraculous'[140] and its fans included Marcel Carné (director of *Le Jour se lève* and *Les Enfants du Paradis*) and Jean Cocteau (poet, artist and director of *La Belle et la Bête*), whom Welles met around this time. The US release was brief and painful; when Richard Wilson, the new manager of Mercury Enterprises, suggested Orson defend the film against the terrible reviews Welles replied that he *cannot imagine what you expect me to write for newspapers beyond simple apology for having been born.*[141]

Macbeth's setbacks had dissuaded Edward Small from funding an *Othello* conceived along similar lines. Alexander Korda aborted the plans for *Cyrano*, by now quite advanced, when he sold the rights to bankroll another project, explaining 'I need the dollars, dear fellow.'[143] Welles secured initial funds for *Othello* from an Italian producer, who then withdrew when he realised Welles was filming Shakespeare not Verdi. Orson shot some footage in Venice, with Lea Padovani as Desdemona. Orson's current inamorata, Padovani offered a whole new perspective on romance. *She treated me like dirt and I had never had that experience. I think I turned . . . into some kind of masochist. I did all the jealous bits! I knew she was humping away*

'Orson Welles is a kind of giant with the look of a child, a tree filled with birds and shadow, a dog that has broken its chain and lies down in the flower beds, an active idler, a wise madman, an island surrounded by people, a pupil asleep in class, a strategist who pretends to be drunk when he wants to be left in peace.'

JEAN COCTEAU[142]

*with other men, and there I was out in the garden looking at the window!
. . . All this happened at a point when I was reaching young middle-age
or elderly youth – I had my comic men's menopause ten years too early, like
everything else!*[144] Orson and Lea had a near-death experience in a
light aircraft and talked of engagement but she eloped with
another crew member. *During the nine months that I spent with her I
paid for everything that I'd ever done to women for 20 years, but in two
days I made her pay for what she did to me in those nine months*[145] was
Welles's grim reckoning. The affair sounds the perfect preparation
for the story of a man driven murderously jealous over his wife's
supposed infidelity.

Over the next two years Welles continued with *Othello* on a
self-funded basis, raising money through acting and shooting a
few scenes whenever he could scrape together a cast and crew – a
less glamorous echo of the era when his radio income funded
Project 891 and the Mercury. One of Orson's acting gigs was as
Cesare Borgia in *Prince of Foxes*, a plodding period romp with
Tyrone Power; again he was the charismatic dastard done in by a
stolid good guy. The location shoot allowed him to surreptitiously
acquire some props and costumes for *Othello*.

Welles also accepted a role in the project for which Korda had
dumped *Cyrano*. Carol Reed – perhaps Britain's leading director
following the success of *Odd Man Out* and his collaboration with
Graham Greene on *The Fallen Idol* – was preparing to shoot another
Greene screenplay, one that offered a character with 'big shoulders
a little hunched, a belly that has known too much good food for
too long, on his face a look of cheerful rascality, a geniality, a
recognition that his happiness will make the world's day.'[146]
Welles immediately recognised that though the part was small,
*every sentence in the whole script is about Harry Lime . . . And then
there's that shot in the doorway – what a star entrance that was!*[147]
It was to prove perhaps the only thoroughly Wellesian role in
which Orson did not direct himself.

The story, *The Third Man*, follows a cowboy writer, Holly Martins, summoned to post-war Vienna by his old pal Harry Lime. Arriving to find him being mourned, Martins' investigations reveal that Lime has staged his own death to escape punishment for black market trading in contaminated antibiotics. That Joseph Cotten was to play Lime's friend and betrayer was an added attraction for Welles. Orson

Cotten and Welles in *The Third Man*

behaved like a prima donna on location in Vienna and then at Shepperton; if he was nervous about working with a talented director rather than a hack – one who might look through his persona rather than contentedly exploit it – he was right. Reed (with Greene) went further than Orson ever had in stripping the magician of his mystique. Performed without the shield of a prosthetic nose, Lime is the very definition of barefaced, a case study in shameless charisma as poisonous contagion.

Lime is visible rather than audible: where Welles always privileged his voice, Reed makes him stand or walk, be observed. That first appearance – when his big, round moon of a face is illuminated into a well-who-did-you-expect? smirk – is mute, as is his pathetic death beneath a barrage of echoing yells. We see him standing on rubble like a colossus astride the Styx but later, sliding into a station café to surprise his pursuers, he is made to loiter shiftily, ignored, almost having to clear his throat to get attention. If Vienna is Lime's stage, the sewers are his backstage, where he plans his entrances and rehearses his lines. He is one more parasitic infection in the guts of a sick city, a pervasive contaminant it can't shift. No wonder he pollutes penicillin – the stuff probably makes

him feel sick. Revealed as a monster, he is hunted down with what look like burning torches. (His pursuers know something that RKO knew when they offered Welles the roles of Quasimodo and Mr Hyde; later one critic called him 'a kind of intellectual Boris Karloff.'[148]) Finally exposed as a shabby grifter, Harry's desperate, wounded eyes show Welles forced into the recognition – and brilliant performance – of an inner self at odds with the showy façade. Could he have created *Touch of Evil*'s Hank Quinlan without this model of smug hypocrisy that collapses, self-defeated, into the mire?

'The sewer is the conscience of the city . . . There, no more false appearances, no plastering over is possible, filth removes its shirt, absolute denudation puts to the rout all illusions and mirages, there is nothing more except what really exists . . . The idea of exploring these leprous regions did not even occur to the police. To try that unknown thing, to cast the plummet into that shadow, to set out on a voyage of discovery in that abyss – who would have dared?'

VICTOR HUGO, *LES MISÉRABLES*

Welles's appearance in *The Third Man* was meant to surprise the audience as much as the characters (on the basis of audience research, the American co-producer David Selznick was keen *not* to use Orson's name in the publicity). Word, of course, got out and, following the film's tremendous critical and popular success, Harry Lime became the role most associated with Welles for the rest of his life: audiences fondly remembered the privilege of being taken into his confidence more than the rotten core it concealed. Though he often begrudged the snubbing of his own films implicit in his association with the role, Orson also described *The Third Man* as *the only movie of mine I ever watch on television because I like it so much*,[149] and happily participated in a spin-off radio series some years later.

Working for Korda also enabled Orson to charge expenses to London Films that in fact went towards preparations for *Othello*. He had persuaded Micheál Mac Liammóir to be his Iago, despite the latter's concerns over his inexperience in the role and before the camera, not to mention his weight (*we'll be two chubby tragedians together*, Welles reassured him[150]). Mac Liammóir's partner Hilton Edwards would be Desdemona's father – once a new actress was found to replace Lea Padovani, that is. Orson had his eye on Cécile Aubry, his co-star in another acting job, *The Black Rose*, in which he was another cunning barbarian. Aubry turned out to be unsuitable; another Desdemona, Betsy Blair, took the role in time for shooting finally to begin in June.

While shooting *The Black Rose* Welles had found a suitably dramatic, windswept 'Cyprus' on the Atlantic coast of Morocco. Mogador (now known as Essaouira) offered 18th-century French ramparts and cannon set against booming surf and sharp, black rock; the light was terrific and the food not at all bad. Imaginative economy was again the prime asset: armour was hammered out of sardine tins and, when costumes were held up in Rome, Welles relocated the murder of Roderigo to a bathhouse (in fact the fish market) and had the cast play it in towels. It was *one of the happiest times I've ever known, despite all the struggle*,[151] he recalled. *We didn't run out of food or wine, or certainly out of talk. We simply ran out of film.*[152] The town remembers its visitor fondly too, with an ornamental Place Orson Welles just outside its perimeter walls – he was, after all, never an insider. There's a relief portrait whose nose, Welles might be gratified to learn, has been struck off or has weathered away.

Place Orson Welles, Essaouira

Welles ditched Betsy Blair and took on yet another Desdemona, Suzanne Cloutier, when filming resumed in Venice in August. The shoot continued in various Moroccan and Italian locations (and French and British studios) for a further year or so. Welles had to remember details of every shot — its countershot (showing the same bit of action from a different angle) might be filmed months later, in a different country. *Every time you see someone with his back turned or a hood over his head, you can be sure it's a stand-in.*[153] Funding was a constant struggle: at one point, in a fit of impoverished extravagance, Orson took a cab from Italy to the south of France to plead for funds from producer Daryl F Zanuck (who agreed, finding the cab fare the first of his obligations).

Welles seems to have pre-empted Bialystock and Bloom in Mel Brooks's film *The Producers* by selling shares in over 100 per cent of the film's profits, perhaps confident it would never make any. If so, it was one of his few shrewd financial calculations. Mac Liammóir and Edwards, mortgaged to the hilt, nearly lost their home, belongings and theatre; Welles wrote to them from Claridge's regretting the lack of available funds. Back in the USA the husk of the Mercury was still fighting off its numerous creditors. In between all this, Orson appeared in comic book form, using magic tricks to help Superman defeat Martian fascists; he signed up (but didn't turn up) for a charity bullfight in Madrid; and he provided an introduction for a book of criticism by a precocious admirer, Kenneth Tynan.

The editing was no easier to fund or quicker to finish than the shoot. Welles had always valued long takes and smooth transitions but had also been alive to the power of editing as a bearer of meaning – *Citizen Kane* is full of witty juxtapositions. The piecemeal *Othello* footage, however, forced Welles to improvise and create in the editing suite as he had never done before – and, for the first time, montage became the foundation of his story. The results were not just convincing

When I'm filming, the sun is the determining factor in something I can't fight against; the actor brings into play something to which I must adapt myself; the story too. I simply arrange things so as to dominate whatever I can . . . One can only take control of a film during editing.[154]

but stunning. On the one hand, Welles exploited the visceral power of editing to convey the mood of a scene: the death of Roderigo, for instance, is composed as violently as he is killed. Few scenes in cinema cut so quick as this death by shards of light, a crescendo of flashing slashes visited on a vulnerable bathing body and set to a high-pitched panic of a score – all a full decade before *Psycho*. On the other hand, Welles also exploited the momentum of an edited scene to distract viewers from its internal inconsistencies: so Iago could step out of a Torcello portico into a Mogador street; Roderigo could land a boot on Cassio's arse in Massaga and be punched back a thousand miles away in Orgete.

But the result is much more than a clever way of papering over the cracks of a ramshackle production. The mélange of locations and juxtaposed images conveys an increasingly dizzying, heady sense of being at the story's mercy. The form is perfectly suited to *Othello*, a tragedy of creative editing and credulous audience. Iago is a master storyteller who weaves circumstantial details into a plausible lie; Othello, caught up in the aggressive momentum of

Iago's montage, quite misses its dodges and elisions. Even Welles's patchwork Desdemona is apt in this context: more even than Charlie Kane, she is a thing of rumour and report, as inconstant to us as she seems to her deluded husband. In convincing us that (at least) three women are one – indeed, that a film cobbled together over four years in as many countries is unfolding, of a piece, before our eyes – Welles goes one better than Iago. Shakespeare's play is a story that warns against story, but Welles's film – so cleverly composed that the viewer can appreciate the full extent of its deception only with detailed knowledge of its production history and the extensive use of a rewind button – demonstrates the strength of our desire to yield to narrative. As it turned out, Welles's *Othello* – this story he was telling – would not find an audience for some time. But he had, eventually, made another film on his terms and, knowing it was possible, condemned himself to many such struggles in future.

Welles with Suzanne Cloutier as Desdemona

That Punch and Judy set 1950–55

As the *Othello* editing was underway, Welles mounted a curious stage medley in Paris, called *The Blessed and the Damned*. The former referred to a new playlet of his called *The Unthinking Lobster*, in which a Hollywood studio becomes a pilgrimage site after the star of a religious picture starts performing genuine miracles. The latter was *Time Runs*, an abbreviated *Faustus* with chunks of Milton and Goethe; the then little-known Eartha Kitt played Helen of Troy, singing Duke Ellington. The June 1950 opening was well reviewed but badly attended, and Orson seemed jealous of Kitt's popularity: on stage he would manoeuvre his bulk to block her miniature frame and one night, when they were to kiss, sank his teeth into her lip and drew blood. They remained friends out of mutual fascination. A slightly different presentation was similarly received in Germany, though Welles disliked the country (and said so). Attempts to film the show failed and, following *The Third Man*'s success, he was besieged by cries of 'Der dritte Mann! Der dritte Mann!'

'When we got there the table was already laid upstairs. He had ordered everything for us from soup to nuts, and everything he had ordered for us naturally he wanted part of . . . He gave me the impression that he wanted a bit of everything . . . So he was sopping up everything he could from us, he was draining us – even those of us like myself who were more or less silent in his company . . . I mean it must have cost a fortune, but I don't think Orson ever paid for anything. He *never* paid the bill!'

EARTHA KITT[155]

Welles and Eartha Kitt in *Time Runs*

The ongoing sagas of *Macbeth* and *Othello* had cemented Orson's image in the US as a lost cause, a dilettante playing pantomime villains for cash and doodling away on self-indulgent pet projects. He was an 'international joke, and possibly the youngest living has-been,' wrote the critic Walter Kerr. 'Welles has let himself turn into a buffoon, and buffoonery is a quality hard to erase from the public mind.'[156]

Perhaps it was partly to counter this that Welles began to drop hints – or at least neglected to discourage suggestions – that his directorial hand could be discerned behind many of the films in which he supposedly only appeared. His legitimate filmic progeny may be few and far between, the argument ran, but the movies are littered with his bastard offspring – as if he were cinematically hyperfertile, unable to set foot on another director's set without creatively cuckolding him.

Invited by Laurence Olivier to mount a stage *Othello*, Welles saw an opportunity to assert his legitimate artistic credentials: *I wanted to play a great classical part in London, and I simply wanted a production that would support it.*[157] In the event Olivier was sniffy about his acting technique in the lead role and the conventional production disappointed aficionados hoping for a touch of Mercury magic in the West End ('Welles has the courage of his restrictions,' sniped Tynan).[158] Generally, however, the show went down well: Welles, growing by the year and massive in a tent-like robe and four-inch heels, must have been like a rumbling, pregnant thundercloud waiting to burst. As usual the cast took the brunt of his emoting: he slammed Desdemona's head against the bedframe one night and bruised Emilia with a faceful of coins. During rehearsals, Orson took on his first steady radio work in years with *The Lives of Harry Lime*. Starting on BBC radio in August 1951, the character's charisma was now pegged to a kind of roguish outlaw decency; a knowing, itinerant cosmopolitan, he was a more comfortable proxy for Orson than Reed and Greene's original whited sepulchre.

Othello was finally ready for the Cannes film festival of May 1952. Entered under the Moroccan flag, Orson's first inkling that it had been well received came when the festival director asked for the Moroccan national anthem; it was duly awarded the Palme d'Or to the strains of *something vaguely Oriental from one of the French operettas*.[159] Despite the accolade, its American release took a further three years. Looking for his next movie idea, Welles returned to an episode from the *Harry Lime* radio series about a secretive, supposedly amnesiac magnate who hires Lime to investigate his own past, only to systematically liquidate the witnesses he tracks down. Orson's script, called *Mr Arkadin*, embellished the concept into a kind of nihilistic reprise of *Citizen Kane*: there the investigation into a great man's life had been absurdly futile;

here it became murderously perilous, with Gregory Arkadin trying to eradicate the past to protect a false present, fearing his beloved daughter will discover his true origins as a white slaver. Orson's old political mentor Louis Dolivet became the picture's producer while Welles appeared in some European pictures to earn cash and wrote *The Lady in the Ice*, a ballet with a chilly view of love that played London and Paris.

Welles backstage in the West End

In August 1953, still awaiting funds for *Arkadin*, Welles spoke at the Edinburgh Festival on the need for a third audience, between populism and elitism. *Here,* he suggested, *television may help us,*[160] even if *the technical excellence of the images in that Punch and Judy set . . . is about as bad as a picture of a Chinese play where they bring on a chair and tell you that it is a mountain.*[161] The new form of mass communication was on his mind. The British theatre director Peter Brook, enjoying success on Broadway, had asked Welles to collaborate on an entry to CBS's prestigious *Omnibus* slot and he was intrigued. The notion of shooting a play in long takes on a single studio soundstage was not new to Orson; André Bazin has noted of his *Macbeth* that 'Welles was in the process of inventing before the fact . . . the technique of directing for television.'[162] And so, having made a deal with the IRS over his outstanding tax, he returned to the US for the first time in five years. Orson had been away during a period of enormous political and cultural movement: he was revolted by McCarthyism – everything his *Free World* editorials had warned against, and now near its apex – but the redbaiters' exploitation of TV was undeniably impressive. He wanted to *find out something about television here. I've never seen an American television show. Television is the one thing this country can't export to Europe.*[163] The medium had grown up in his absence, with the likes of *Studio One, Actors' Studio* and *Omnibus* showing accomplished, socially engaged dramas.

Welles and Brook decided to present *King Lear*, the story of a man, like Arkadin, trying to hold onto his power and his daughter's love. Still only 38, Welles was keen as ever to embrace geriatric roles. Slashed to 74 minutes, the play was shown without ads, maintaining Orson's principle of avoiding intervals. Their version of the text excised the plotlines revolving around Gloucester and Edgar (although the 'Poor Tom' scenes remained, with Micheál Mac Liammóir charismatically antic in the part). The setting was fairly traditional, with a limited number of castle and 'outdoor' sets; like Orson's film of *Macbeth*, Brook's production used long takes with fluid transitions between them and soliloquies were spoken to camera.

Welles absorbed as much technical knowledge about television as he could; for once his behaviour was impeccably polite, his occasional foot-stamping reserved for matters of artistic perfectionism. *Technologically, television is a hundred years ahead of film,*[164] he enthused. Of the October 18 broadcast, *Cue* magazine said: 'Like a confidently patient boxer who lets his opponent flail away for eight or nine rounds and then calmly steps in to finish the fight with one blow, Orson Welles burst into television . . . and knocked everything for a loop. The performance he gave as King Lear established a new high for the medium in terms of power, heart and sheer artistry.'[165] Welles's biographer Frank Brady notes the audience of 15 million was 'more than all the people put together who had seen the play since it was written'[166] and letters of praise came in.

Orson was keen to follow up on the success. The network suggested further *Omnibus* specials and even held talks with Welles on a $3 million six-part series with star actors. But the network did not much like Orson's ideas or he theirs, and the idea was eventually dropped. It was perhaps the greatest missed opportunity of his later career. Given the originality of the TV programmes he would eventually make, a series created by Orson Welles in 1953 could have proved as innovative and influential on that form as any of his earlier creations for the theatre, radio and film were on theirs – indeed, his achievements in those fields had left their own mark on television. His radio 'The War of the Worlds', for instance, clearly influenced a simulation of a nuclear attack on New York in *See It Now* (1952) while another TV series, *First Person Singular* (1952–3), used the camera-as-character form that Orson had conceived for *Heart of Darkness*. Had Welles been in charge of the *Kraft Television Theater*, *Studio One* or the *Philco and Goodyear Television Playhouses* – all popular drama showcases running in this period – he might have taken the medium down fruitful pathways and even forged contacts with a new generation of film-makers: Marlon Brando, Robert Altman, Arthur Penn, Sam Peckinpah and Rod Steiger all worked on them. Even then, however, the balance was beginning to shift from experimentation towards the profitable formula programming that would by the 1960s have established a stranglehold on network television. By the time of Orson's most concerted efforts to break into the medium a few years later, the opportunity had passed.

By the beginning of 1954 enough funds were in place to start work on *Mr Arkadin*. Welles of course played the hollow man; Robert Arden, from the *Harry Lime* radio show, was his patsy-nemesis Van Stratten, the grifter employed to exhume his past. Akim Tamiroff, Michael Redgrave and Mischa Auer were among Arkadin's former contacts; and for his daughter Raina, Welles cast his lover Paola Mori. She was half his age and Countess di Girfalco, the daughter of an Italian colonial administrator imprisoned under Mussolini. This leftist aristocratic background had appealed to both the progressive and the nostalgist in Welles when they met a couple of years previously; her beauty and wit did the rest and she was soon a regular guest at the *Othello* locations.

Orson filmed Van Stratten's globetrotting mission over the next eight months in Munich, Paris, Rome and various Spanish locations (a Spanish-language version was made simultaneously), occasionally excusing himself for acting work. Arden, with whom he picked a bitter argument before tearfully apologising, thought him 'the most gifted fourteen-year-old I've ever known,'[167] but another cast member, Frederic O'Brady, remembered him working 'quietly like a man who is sure of what he's doing. As far as I know, his only outbursts are laughs, and they are big loud, healthy laughs.'[168] Post-production proved lengthy. A few years later, Welles confessed that *in the editing room I work very slowly, which always enrages the producers who tear the film from my hands. I don't know why it takes me so long. I could work for an eternity editing a film.*[169]

When he missed a Christmas 1954 deadline for the Venice film festival, Dolivet passed control to an editor beyond Orson's supervision. Having once considered proposing Welles as secretary-general of the United Nations, Dolivet now found him aggressively temperamental and launched a $700,000 lawsuit on behalf of *Arkadin*'s backers, citing Orson's drunkenness and the casting of Mori as contrary to the film's interests. (Eventually settled out of court, the case delayed the film's US release until 1962.) The eventual result is a film known by at least two names (it is sometimes called *Confidential Report*) that exists in half a dozen different versions, many without the crucial framing narrative. This might have appealed to Gregory Arkadin's rejection of stable, consistent identity but Welles insisted *they completely destroyed the movie! More completely than any other picture of mine has been hurt by anybody, Arkadin was destroyed because they completely changed the entire form of it . . . Ambersons is nothing compared to Arkadin!*[170]

Where *Citizen Kane* gave us a man whose icy shell could not be penetrated, Arkadin is only surface, an empty façade: you can literally see the joins in Welles's make-up. The film's structure is similarly superficial: where Kane gives us a prismatic account of its lead's personality, *Arkadin*'s paper-chase offers an entertaining rogue's gallery but no purchase on the man himself. Ultimately, at the lightest of touches – the mere thought of his past being exposed to his daughter – he disappears from his private plane, vanishing in mid-air like the soap bubble he is. As a sinister master of revels at a masked ball, Arkadin recounts a famous fable about a frog who agrees to carry a scorpion across a river on condition that the scorpion will not sting him. Mid-stream, the scorpion stings the frog anyway, condemning them both to drown. 'It's my character,' the scorpion shrugs. Arkadin – and the Welles persona in general – is usually assumed to be the scorpion, but isn't there something froglike too about Welles's self-destructive showmen, about the way he invites Van Stratten's prying, just as Lime courts Holly Martins' betrayal? The magician needs the cleverness of his tricks to be recognised – even if it destroys him.

As well as recalling Kane, Arkadin in many ways set the template for the characters Welles would play in most of his remaining films: great, hollow men who fear yet incite the collapse of their own legend. Key to this is his treatment of these characters' voices: in his early movies Welles often privileged his characters' speech over their physical presence to let the power of their words achieve maximum impact. In his later works, he increasingly uses this separation to signal their hubris and inevitable defeat. We often hear from Arkadin by telephone, for instance; he almost seems able to cross the globe on its wires. Yet at the airport, his bellowing for a ticket does him no good; nor does his last attempt to avert catastrophe, when he sends his disembodied voice booming down from his private plane: 'My daughter's somewhere at the airport. Bring her to the radio at once!' It's the desperation of a radio performer in fear of losing his audience; able to seduce anyone who gives their ear, he is undone by her simple claim that she knows the truth – the ultimate defeat for a magician or actor. The voice falls silent.

When released in Europe in 1955, *Mr Arkadin* found admirers, usually on the basis of its obliqueness and artificiality. *Cahiers du Cinéma* critic and New Wave director Eric Rohmer praised its creation of 'an exceptional world, which we believe in all the more because it is presented as exceptional'[171] while on its eventual US release *Film Culture* greeted it as 'a relief from the literalness of most pictures . . . the spectator cannot 'sit back and relax' but must meet the film at least half-way to try to figure out what the hell is going on.'[172]

The observer of Welles's career over the coming years requires a similar degree of concentration. Immediately after finishing shooting *Mr Arkadin*, Welles shot some test footage in Paris with two of its cast, Mischa Auer and Akim Tamiroff, as Don Quixote and Sancho Panza. Cervantes's classic novel about a decrepit, impoverished country squire who fancies himself a chivalric knight errant had obvious appeal for Orson (apart from his life-long fascination with Spanish culture): its sophisticated narrative structure is used to explore the seductive power of story itself, while its knowing but sympathetic approach to deluded idealism can't have helped but strike a chord after the adventures of *Othello* and *Arkadin*. This particular test came to nothing but the lunatic knight would prove an intermittent diversion throughout the last three decades of Welles's life. The parallels between Quixote's escapades and Welles's own frustrated zeal would only become more painfully apt.

Adventures on a small screen 1955–56

As *Mr Arkadin* was taking shape in late 1954, Welles had flown from Paris – where he was living with Paola – to London to appear in John Huston's film of *Moby Dick*. Orson got on terrifically with Huston and executed his cameo as Father Mapple with ease, delivering a moving sermon from a prow-like pulpit to a congregation of 'shipmates'. By the following February Welles was planning his own stage version of the story. Perhaps conscious that mounting a plausible whale hunt on stage was the mission of a monomaniac like Ahab rather than a mere egomaniac like himself, Orson imagined a 19th-century theatre troupe who were in the process of rehearsing their own *Moby Dick*. He dubbed this typically sophisticated narrative experiment *Moby Dick – Rehearsed*. In keeping with the self-referential script, the stage was to be *interestingly and even romantically dressed with all the lumber of an old-fashioned theater*.[173] The setting is revealing. Welles claimed never to be happier than when rehearsing in an empty auditorium – *the moment people are let in it loses some of its magic*.[174]

Orson of course would play the troupe's actor-manager or 'Governor', whose roles were Ahab and Mapple – another formal excuse for acting at arm's length, and for self-parody. 'What exactly do you want me to do?' the Serious Actor asks. 'Do?' booms the Governor. 'Stand six feet away and do your damnedest!'[175] Welles's British writer friend Wolf Mankowitz (no relation to his *Kane* co-author Herman Mankiewicz) helped secure a London venue and casting began. Patrick McGoohan played that Serious Actor and the young Joan Plowright was the girl who plays the cabin boy. Kenneth Williams, whose vocal dexterity was bringing success in radio comedy, was also cast.

Wolf Mankowitz also had contacts at the BBC, with whom Welles had had happy radio experiences, and who now offered him a cheap TV show. *Orson Welles's Sketch Book* would feature anecdotes delivered straight to camera, illustrated with occasional sketches by the man himself. In 1938 he had said of radio that *the listeners should be considered as small groups of two or three, and then the idea of intimacy can be best achieved . . . When a fellow leans back in his chair and begins: 'Now, this is how it happened' the listener feels that the narrator is taking him into his confidence; he begins to take a personal interest in the outcome.*[176] On television Orson could add nods, winks and twinkles to that vocal rapport. He seduced the camera as easily as he had the microphone, addressing it like an old friend. The six quarter-hours – running weekly from 24 April 1955, during *Moby Dick* rehearsals – touched on such topics as false noses, *It's All True*, diplomatic bureaucracy, Houdini, 'The War of the Worlds' and autocues (*in this particular show, of course, I don't need a prompt as I make it up as I go along*). A tremendous success, it confirmed Welles's fascination with the television form.

On 6 May 1955, the boy wonder turned 40 and, two days later, married the woman to whom he would remain happily (if not monogamously) married for the rest of his life. 'It is not that Orson is abnormal,' Paola – now 24 and pregnant – told the *Daily Express*. 'He is supernormal. The secret is finding out how normal he is underneath the super.'[177]

Moby Dick – Rehearsed opened on 16 June, reaping the usual mix of besotted and sceptical reviews; the *Evening Standard* thought it 'a very good radio play.' Welles made changes throughout the run, even improvising in performance: sometimes, recalled Gordon Jackson (Ishmael), 'he'd go all out, and find himself at the end of a limb, with egg dripping down his face. Other nights, he absolutely soared, and was *magnificent!*'[178] One night his false nose peeled off; other nights he hissed *self-pity!* at actors he thought were overdoing it. He was delighted with the show – *the best thing I ever did in any form*[179] – and also with London, where, unlike Broadway, *they take plays and actors seriously.*[180] There was an unfortunate chance encounter with John Houseman, now thriving as a movie producer; they didn't meet again for a quarter century.

Welles filmed over an hour of *Moby Dick – Rehearsed* with a view to proposing it to CBS's *Omnibus*, which had screened *King Lear*, but he aborted the enterprise dissatisfied. Rather than extend the play's run, he accepted an offer from British commercial television to make a series of travelogues broadcast that summer. Further developing his direct flirtation with the lens, *Around the World with Orson Welles* also showcased his genuinely curious appetite for travel and increasingly sophisticated grasp of television grammar. In many ways it was a series of essays developing interests that had been evident as early as *It's All True*, or indeed his trips to China and Ireland. The episode on the Basque country presented a romanticised paean to an ancient people with a strongly personalised narration. He returned to Harry Lime's Vienna, and presented a witty montage of Paris, all cats, cafés and schoolkids. There were leisurely interviews with Chelsea pensioners and almshouse residents in London, in which Welles proved himself as good a listener as a raconteur, and aired his long-considered views on ageing. His complex yet unobtrusive editing technique combined interview footage with reaction shots filmed later (now standard practice) and frequent glances at the camera, as if checking that the third participant in these conversations – the audience – was still engaged.

By contrast, in the episode on Spanish bullfighting he almost became a character in his own show: Kenneth Tynan and his wife Elaine Dundy presented, Welles appearing only to commentate on the fight itself. The programme's violence upset many viewers, but it was the last edition – an investigation into the infamous murder of the British Drummond family in a French Alpine village the previous year – that provoked the most controversy. An elderly farmer had been convicted and the story of an old man accused by his own sons must have caught Welles's eye for intimate betrayals. His report was one of the first for TV to use synchronised sound recording, handheld footage in a simulation of a physical attack and the now-familiar trope of locating the interviewer's shoulder in shot while the subject speaks. Shot as a new inquiry was launched, it was perhaps too contentious to show at the time and was never completed.

Plans to take *Moby Dick* to the Gate in Dublin faltered, as did the idea of a Shakespeare repertory season on Broadway. Orson did find backing, however, for a *King Lear* at the cavernous New York City Center and Orson arrived that October *to present my credentials as a classical theater man to a new generation of New York playgoers*.[181] His hopes of creating a new Mercury (or something like it) were short-lived: his British cast were denied entry visas and their replacements preferred to work to union regulations rather than in all-night marathons. Why weren't they excited at the adventure of it all? He had *a feeling of being in a foreign land – which I hadn't felt being in foreign lands*.[182] Funding proved more slippery than expected too. No longer the preening lion cub, Welles bore too many scars, had grown too saggy around the jowls; he provoked a kind of morbid curiosity rather than faith in his limitless potential. Now he was expected to account for and justify everything he did. *Promises*, he noted much later, *are more fun than explanations*.[183] The birth on 13 November 1955 of a new daughter – named for Orson's mother – was some consolation. As Barbara Leaming notes, 'it is oddly fitting that Beatrice should be born just as he was preparing *Lear*; in a sense she would be his Cordelia, the beloved youngest of three daughters.'[184]

Rehearsals for the ambitious *Lear* continued as best they could until, a week before the premiere, Orson broke his ankle. Limping through the previews, he injured the other ankle on opening night (12 January 1956) and appeared at the next performance in a wheelchair, begging the audience to stay for some readings and anecdotes. He brought the house lights up as if to foster or demand collaboration. Even though, as he had reminded *Sketch Book* viewers mere months before, *an audience is not necessarily a group of friendly well-wishers*, he asked them to look kindly on this . . . what, *King Lear – Rehearsed?* After all, they were still getting the spectacle of a play being attempted. Critically savaged, the run laboured on for 21 shows, Lear wheeled by his fool, and lost $60,000; it would be Orson's last appearance on the New York stage. There were a few dissenting voices amidst the general drubbing, offering mercy to a man damned by his reputation. 'Was there not,' wondered *Commonweal*'s Richard Hayes, 'something punishing and harsh in the meager critical and popular response to Mr Welles's elaborate production? How do we make the prodigy pay for his early audacities, long after he has sloughed them off!'[185]

Following this experience, Orson made for the profitable consolations of vaudeville, playing a successful six-week run of conjuring, gags and Shakespeare at the Riviera Hotel, Las Vegas. Then in April 1956, he, Paola and Beatrice relocated to Hollywood, where – out of both interest and, given his inability to launch features, necessity – the bulk of Welles's attention went to TV. He had appeared several times on CBS while in New York. Now he played a great ham opposite Betty Grable in *Twentieth Century* and guested on *I Love Lucy*. This collaboration led to another offer from Lucille Ball's company, Desilu, which was based on the old RKO lot. Presumably conscious of the current smash TV show *Alfred Hitchcock Presents*, and realising they had the only other director with a comparable public profile, they proposed a similar idea: Orson would produce, write, direct and present a series of

Orson with Paola and Beatrice, his family

The poverty of television is marvellous. Clearly a great classic film will be bad on a small screen, because television is an enemy to the values of classic film, but not to film itself. It's a marvellous form, the spectator is only five feet from the screen. But television isn't a dramatic form, it's a narrative form, the ideal form of expression for a storyteller . . . I prefer stories to dramas, to plays, to novels. It's an important aspect of my taste.[186]

stories. You only have to compare the pilot episode of Welles's experimental concoction to *Hitchcock*'s budget noir to see the difference between someone seriously engaging with TV's formal potential and someone cashing in on his brand name.

Adapted from a John Collier short story, 'The Fountain of Youth' concerns concerned a middle-aged scientist who uses his experiments into eternal youth to drive a wedge between his Broadway starlet fiancée and her tennis ace lover. It's a tongue-in-cheek take on many of Welles's established concerns: gossip, reputation and, in particular, ageing. *Almost all of us wish we were just a little younger than we are*, smirks the man who spent decades in pursuit of preternatural maturity. But the telling is more extraordinary than the tale. Welles uses conspicuously artificial backdrops and back projection, so that with a change of lighting and a couple of props the scene shifts from a quayside to a restaurant without the actors ever leaving the camera's gaze. This was not entirely new to television, but Welles's narratorial control was: wandering through the story in black tie, he conducts and comments on its progress, even stops it in its tracks. Sometimes stills, silhouettes or drawings illustrate his narration; sometimes the characters are literally his mouthpieces, miming to lines he speaks. There are moments, of course, when we hear his voice over a black screen.

The pilot came in a little behind schedule and over budget; the question of Welles's reliability was never far away. But it was the failure to find a sponsor that did for its chances: though fertile subjects for Orson, ageing, vanity and bitterness were hardly the stuff of network dreams. As Welles would write of Hollywood a few years later, *the industrial system, by its nature, cannot accommodate originality. A genuine individual is an outright nuisance in a factory.*[187] He continued to experiment with the medium and pour his own money into his projects, a sure sign of his passion. For a projected series of television biographies, using many of the techniques of *Around the World with Orson Welles*, Orson made a programme illustrated with his own drawings about Alexandre Dumas *in a purely narrative form, but quite visual in spite of that. Nobody would have any part of it.*[188] The series was also to to have included Barnum and Churchill, but was never picked up. 'The Fountain of Youth' was finally aired in September 1958 in a graveyard slot for unoptioned pilots, to substantial praise. The *World-Telegram and Sun* suggested 'should an eager young chap from one of those opinion surveys corner you and ask, "What, in your judgment, does television need right now?" look him straight in his avid eye and say, "Orson Welles."'[189] It won a Peabody Award for excellence but by then Welles's hopes of a Hollywood TV career were over.

The frustrations of these failed personal projects were both mitigated and compounded by acting jobs that increasingly represented Welles's only public profile (as well as servicing his still-substantial tax burden). One role, as a cattle baron for producer Albert Zugsmith, yielded more satisfying results: in late 1956 Zugsmith asked him to play another heavy, the shady cop in Universal's *Badge of Evil*, a pretty ordinary script based on a recent novel. Charlton Heston was the good guy. There are several accounts of what happened next, but the upshot was that as well as starring, Welles was contracted to rewrite and direct the picture – his first in the US for a decade.

With renewed optimism he compiled for his daughter Rebecca, now aged 12, an exquisite Christmas present, a picture book based on St Tropez's annual festival of Les Bravades. It offered both beautiful illustrations and a chatty, discursive paean to the processions

An image from *Les Bravades*

and carnivals that played key parts in such diverse Welles projects as *Too Much Johnson*, *Don Quixote* and *Mr Arkadin*. *I've been to such events in Sicily and China, in southern Spain and Italy and on the Alti-Plano of Bolivia*, he wrote of the French festivities. *I've seen things as beautiful and true in this line, but absolutely nothing as completely and utterly unlike anything else on earth. And never anything as serious and gay at the same time.* That could almost be a description of the film he was about to make: *Touch of Evil* (as Welles renamed it), though not exactly gay, was shot through with gallows humour even as it offered the most serious-minded consideration of ethical behaviour he had yet put on screen.

Some kind of man 1956–60

In his BBC *Sketch Book*, Orson had noted that *it's the essence of our society that a policeman's job should be hard. He's there to protect the free citizen, not to chase criminals. That's an incidental part of the job.* His new screenplay was a meditation on this theme, adapted from both the original novel and Universal's initial script. The basic story – in which a young detective and his wife are jeopardised when he investigates the suspect practices of an influential police-man, Hank Quinlan – remained the same but Welles increased its ethnic tension and sense of outlandish grotesquery. He relocated the action to a border town and made the younger man a Mexican called Vargas (even though Heston already had the role); there were new scenes at a remote motel manned by a skittish clerk, the role of the hoodlum Joe Grandi was beefed up and Welles created an old flame for Quinlan, a gypsy madam called Tanya, played by his old friend Marlene Dietrich. Vargas and Quinlan were made more clearly good and bad, and Quinlan's reputation – rather than the fate of Sanchez, the young man he frames for murder, or the plight of Vargas's imperilled wife Susan – became the crux of the plot. Like Arkadin, Quinlan sees his substantial achievements and reputation threatened by a young man's investigation into his dubious past.

Welles assembled a company including several old friends and collaborators. As well as Dietrich, Akim Tamiroff (from *Arkadin* and *Don Quixote*) played Grandi and Joseph Cotten gave a cameo; the director of photography was Russell Metty, who had worked

'You're a mess, honey.' Welles as
Detective Hank Quinlan

on *Ambersons* and *The Stranger*, while *Kane*'s Maurice Seiderman provided Welles's gross Quinlan make-up. The old gang mentality was reinforced by location shooting at Venice Beach; Janet Leigh (Susan) said the studio 'really didn't know what was happening.'[190] The shoot went almost too smoothly: at one point, when the wind turned and ruined continuity, Orson bellowed *You've got it going the wrong way!*[191] and it duly changed back. The cast all testified to his constructive attention and for once he even found his own part a cinch.

Welles had never gone so far in making himself physically grotesque, with sagging jowls, bleary, baggy eyes and padding added to his already sizeable bulk. 'You're a mess, honey,' Tanya deadpans. 'You should lay off those candy bars.'

Quinlan is a self-portrait, but not simply self-mocking. He is a man who gets results despite his inability to function within institutional rules, who magically knows guilt like Welles intuitively knew the precise spot to place his camera – each is a master framer. If Arkadin and *Arkadin* were fragile, overstretched facades, Quinlan and *Touch of Evil* are foetid through and through. Yet this rancid fever dream never loses its humorous undertow. There's an absurd edge even to the most terrifying moments (Susan's motel room ordeal, Grandi's Grand Guignol demise), a frisson of doubt about whether you are appalled at the horror or the bad taste of it all. Metty's exaggerated, wide-angle photography is ominous yet almost cartoonish, and the comic acting terrific: Mr and Mrs Vargas are the hapless straight men to Welles's monstrous lawman, Tamiroff's hood with a toupee and Dennis Weaver's nervy motel clerk. (This last character, strikingly similar to Norman Bates, gave Leigh the chance to rehearse for *Psycho*, still two years away.)

Status and voice are prominent as ever: Quinlan and Vargas, both proud men, recognise that one will lose his reputation. Susan's ordeal starts with a spooky voice whispering through the walls ('you know what the boys are trying to do, don't you?') and when it is over, Vargas is positively Ambersonian in thinking of her 'good name' almost before her security. 'Our local police celebrity', meanwhile, has long expected his word to be proof against scepticism but his words are what undo him. In an early sequence he lays out the apparently incontrovertible charges against a suspect from off-screen, but that same disembodied voice will damn Quinlan himself when he is unwittingly bugged at the end. There's something horribly compulsive about him standing on that bridge, transfixed by the sound of his own voice echoing from the transistor below, just as Othello had eavesdropped on Iago and Cassio's conversation like a rapt radio listener. As Vargas – Quinlan's Macduff – tells him, 'this is finally something you can't talk your way out of.' Tanya's famous last line – 'He was some kind of man. What does it matter what you say about people?' – is a small mercy, an offhand rejection of the maelstrom of gossip and reputation that finally sucked Quinlan into that stinking river. It's as generous as Anna's sentiments about Harry Lime ('a person doesn't change because you find out more') or Sophie's about Arkadin ('he's going to so much trouble to be someone else, why should I spoil it for him?'). *Nothing could be more vulgar than to worry about posterity*,[192] Welles once said; *it is just another version of success, which is always rightly suspect*.[193]

Vargas and Quinlan stand off

After the final take, early on the morning of 2 April 1957, Welles and Heston went for bacon, eggs and champagne. There was much to celebrate in their work and post-production started well: young Henry Mancini's threatening rock 'n' roll music and nostalgic pianola motif made for a score that was both loaded with emotional cues and integral to the action while the cutting, after a false start with an unsympathetic editor, progressed reasonably well. After two months' work Universal, perhaps impatient with Orson's perfectionism, imposed a new editor who was to work alone, although Welles sent frequent memoranda. At the end of June, however, Welles absented himself, travelling to Mexico for a rest holiday (he may have had some kind of nervous exhaustion) and to work on *Don Quixote*. Cash had become available for a short TV version of the story; Welles wanted Heston but he had other commitments so Tamiroff's Panza was joined by the Spanish actor Francisco Reiguera (a dead ringer for the established image of the Don), and Patty McCormack as the young girl to whom Welles, as himself, recounts the story. Shooting was fast, confident and imaginative. Relocating the knight and squire to contemporary society, Orson highlighted the anachronism of the Don's behaviour (the novel's main joke but one often lost on 20th-century audiences): Quixote railed against the cinema and delighted in mechanical earth-movers. At night Welles dubbed the narration and both leads; when funds ran out he wept, claiming to lack only 15 of the planned 90 minutes.

Meanwhile, a fourth editor – Ernest Nims – had taken over *Touch of Evil* and streamlined the narrative. *Jokes and morals went*,[194] Welles noted after viewing the new cut at the end of August. As with *The Lady from Shanghai* he found it frustrating trying to convince the studio that certain elements were *deliberately intended to create a certain bewilderment*.[195] But he also told Nims one re-edited scene was *not only superior to what it was at the stage when I left it, but actually better than the effect I'd been hoping for*.[196] There was more *Quixote* in September and October, and Welles also went to Louisiana to act in *The Long, Hot Summer*. Meanwhile Universal decided they needed additional shots for *Touch of Evil* and, reportedly unable to contact Welles, had a studio employee shoot them approximating his style. When he finally viewed this latest version, Welles submitted another long memo; as before, about half of his suggested changes were adopted. The film as released was, yet again, not the cut Welles had envisaged but despite outraged letters written to Leigh and especially Heston at the time of the reshoots (*UNLESS THE STUDIO IS STOPPED THEY ARE GOING TO WRECK OUR PICTURE – AND I MEAN WRECK IT*[197]), Orson later grudgingly granted that the story was still roughly *intact when they were finished*.[198]

The production history did Welles's reputation no favours and, released without press screenings or publicity in February 1958, *Touch of Evil* received mixed notices: *Variety* said it 'smacked of brilliance and ultimately flounders in it.'[200] By then, however, Orson, Paola and Beatrice had sailed for Genoa, settling in Italy for the foreseeable future. *Touch of Evil* went

'It's accepted wisdom that Orson deserved better of the film industry than he got; it is also true that the film industry deserved better of Orson than it got . . . I mean, he can charm actors and stage hands and drivers and make-up people; why can't he take a little time and charm the men who are going to give him the money to make the movies?'

Charlton Heston[199]

down well in Europe: a two-week showing in Paris was extended through the winter and the Brussels World Fair gave it two awards. Truffaut's reading was more understanding than any American review: 'Welles preaches to his parishioners and seems to be clearly telling us: I'm sorry I'm slovenly; it's not my fault if I'm a genius; I'm dying: love me.'[201] Welles told *Cahiers du Cinéma* that he was thinking of quitting the movies. *I need to find another, cheaper means of expression – like this tape recorder!*[202] he said, perhaps already suspecting that the interview itself might become his preferred form. He worked on a TV pilot – ultimately rejected – for ABC called 'Portrait of Gina', an interview essay about Gina Lollobrigida in which her image and persona received as much attention as the woman herself. Developing his self-reflexive style – cutaways filmed later, shots of camera equipment – it was also one of the first appearances of the broad-brimmed hat, cape and cigar that characterised Orson's image in his later years.

Being in show business today is like being a cherry picker, he told reporters. *We go where the crops are.*[203] So he narrated bad widescreen epics, acted again for John Huston and appeared in a handful of European mediocrities. There was one role that allowed him to impress: the lawyer in *Compulsion*, Richard Fleischer's version of the 1924 Leopold and Loeb case. Fleischer was wary of Welles, whom he thought envious of his position. 'You really have to feel your way for a while to see whether you can direct him or whether he's going to direct you. He knows so damn much. He knows what you're doing before you think of it yourself . . . You have to gain his confidence. If he has no confidence in you, he will steam-roller you, flatten you right out.'[204] The cornerstone of the role was a 12-minute courtroom speech against capital punishment that Welles delivered with all the rhetorical skill and passion of his 1944 political broadcasts. As with Father Mapple in *Moby Dick*, having an on-screen audience for his character removed the need for competitive histrionics sometimes evident in Welles's performances. Guaranteed his viewers' undivided attention, he could use his charisma to cool rather than inflame, to provoke thought rather than demand amazement.

Hilton Edwards invited Orson to Ireland to mount a Shakespeare that could raise much-needed funds for all involved. Returning to his *Five Kings* history amalgam, Welles worked from *Henry IV* parts 1 and 2, *Henry V* and *The Merry Wives of Windsor* and focused in on the triangle between Henry IV, his dissolute son Hal and Hal's roguish drinking companion Sir John Falstaff, who is cast out when Hal inherits the throne. The notions of rival fathers and filial rejection were still live for Orson 30 years after Dick's death and his choice between Skipper and Dadda. To Welles, Falstaff was *the character in which I most believe, the most entirely good man of all dramatic literature. His faults are minimal, and he derives the most enormous pleasure from them. His goodness is like bread, like wine.*[205] This perhaps says more about Welles than about Shakespeare's conniving knight who, as well as a good companion, is an incorrigible debtor, stealer of credit and user of friends; like Don Quixote, he is a selfish liability as well as hugely entertaining. Orson had a strong affinity with this canny performer condemned to self-pitying exile, this shameless self-promoter born with a white beard whose catch-all excuse – ''tis my vocation, Hal' – is another version of Arkadin's 'it's my character'. The cold new order's rejection of Falstaff resonated with Welles. He longed for the days when actors *were royal bums . . . Our crown was tin, but it was a crown, and we wore it, with a difference, among such other diadems as happened to be gold.*[206] Orson's Falstaff was a man no less worthy of love and respect because he was *obliged to sing for his supper . . . It's not that he was funny; he had to be funny.*[207]

After Dublin, *Chimes at Midnight* – as Orson named his composition – was to go to London, then Europe, then perhaps – like *Macbeth* – onto film. A young actor called Keith Baxter, who had an aptly Welsh and military background, played Hal, and Orson

'When Welles laughed, he started slowly, cocking an eye towards his companion, watching his response. When the response was encouraging (how could it not be?), the laugh swelled and began to gather force, like a typhoon, until his features were dissolved into a mask of Falstaffian delight. Still, the laugh was ingratiating, not intimidating, for Welles kept a slight portion of that eye fixed on his companion.'

Joseph McBride[208]

directed largely by telephone from around Europe. With barely a week's proper rehearsals, the production wasn't as polished as it might have been; running for a week in Belfast from 13 February 1960 then a month in Dublin, it was well enough reviewed but poorly attended. As hopes of a London transfer evaporated, Welles lost interest, though he told Baxter to await a summons to reprise the role on film.

Two opportunities arose around this time, one theatrical, one cinematic, neither on familiar territory. One night Olivier came to *Chimes at Midnight*; Welles was soon signed on to direct the London premiere of Eugène Ionesco's parable of thoughtless totalitarianism, *Rhinoceros*, with Olivier as Berenger, the lone everyman holding out against the growing herd. Like Quixote or Falstaff, Berenger finds himself a righteous relic of a bygone age. For the first time since *Ambersons*, Welles would direct without performing, but while in 1942 that arrangement had been the *joy of my life*,[209] this was an unhappy experience. Despite the technical pleasures of the production, Welles increasingly disliked

Rhinoceros as a play and claimed that Olivier *made it almost impossible for me to direct the cast. He got them off in little groups and had little quiet rehearsals having nothing to do with me.*[210] For once, rather than lecturing other directors on their sets, Orson was upstaged on his own. Moreover, after decades of over-indulgence Welles's health was growing chronically bad and *Chimes'* failure had added to his substantial financial woes (Edwards and Mac Liammóir threatened to sue). Orson absented himself for a few days prior to *Rhinoceros*'s 28 April opening before attending the heavily publicised opening and making last-minute refinements. Having rigged up a microphone to instruct the crew and even cast during performance, his commands were apparently audible to the audience – was Welles refusing to let his directorial voice go unheard?

The run went well but Welles didn't participate in its West End transfer or get attractive job offers as a result. He had, however, been in discussions with Alexander Salkind, who had produced one of the European films he'd appeared in. The possibility of Welles making a film for Salkind had arisen and, after a false start or two, the producer sent a list of literary properties for Welles to choose from. None leapt out at him but he eventually selected *The Trial*. Orson was no more constitutionally sympathetic to Kafka's sensibility than to Ionesco's but the perverted investigation was familiar territory and the idea of a wilful individual at odds with institutional authority appealed to something fundamental in him. *I've had recurring nightmares of guilt all my life: I'm in prison and I don't know why . . .* [*The Trial is*] *much closer to my own feelings about everything than any other picture I've ever made.*[211]

The fragile king 1960–70

*'You felt that there was a great deal of him in Falstaff –
this sort of trimming one's sails, always short of money,
having to lie, perhaps, and to cheat.'*

Keith Baxter

Although Europe had had its share of disappointments –
Rhinoceros being the latest – it had over the previous dozen years
offered a more generally sympathetic climate than Orson's home-
land. Now, however, his reputation at home was undergoing
something of a reassessment. In 1961 a young writer named Peter
Bogdanovich organised an extensive retrospective of Welles's
career at the New York Museum of Modern Art, and a new
generation of cinephiles was rediscovering *Citizen Kane* (which the
following year was voted best film ever in *Sight and Sound*, a
position it has held in the magazine's ten-yearly critics' poll ever
since). Welles's critical reputation would steadily grow over
the last two decades of his life, but this never aided the various
projects for which he was invariably chasing funds.

The most pressing of these hoped-for schemes was currently
Don Quixote. Having made a successful pitch to Italian TV,
Orson departed for Spain in early 1961 to make an eight-part
travelogue, *In the Land of Don Quixote*, in which he, Paola
and Beatrice explored the nation and its history while he shot
scenes for his Cervantes feature. Now rejecting much of
the Mexican footage, Welles was constantly revising his idea

of the project, which was never to be finalised in his mind, let alone as a complete print.

One film was, however, fully budgeted and set to proceed: shooting on *The Trial* began in Paris in March 1962. If Susan Vargas was Janet Leigh's preparation for *Psycho*'s Marion Crane, Joseph K allowed Anthony Perkins to reprise the fussy neuroses and malapropisms of Norman Bates as, in his prim, priggish way, he fruitlessly tries to establish the nature of the charges against him and his means of defence. Welles appeared as the pompous, unhelpful Advocate (*there was no other actor of my calibre I could afford*[213]) and Tamiroff was his timorous client. Romy Schneider, Elsa Martinelli and Jeanne Moreau – who would become one of Orson's regular players – played the three women whose sexuality so perturbs K. Welles's funding suddenly fell through before his monumental sets could be built. Serendipitously he came across the Gare d'Orsay – formerly one of Paris's major stations, at that time abandoned, later to become its modern art museum – whose cavernous spaces provided perfect sets for Kafka's bureaucracy and ample office space for the production to boot. *It was really one of those moments like the Turkish bath in Othello. In one case no costumes; in the other, no sets.*[214]

Welles used the cunning geographical elisions he pioneered in *Othello* to stitch together the fruits of a 10-week shoot that crisscrossed Italy and Yugoslavia, whose unusual landscape and brutalist architecture suited Welles's conception. In one sequence Perkins leaves an Orsay office set, walks down the steps of a Roman palazzo, past a Milanese factory and into a Zagreb interior. Welles's editing underpins the film's dreamlike feel: doors unexpectedly connect a grand public hall and a squalid punishment cupboard, a rickety artist's garret and a geometric room of archived files. *The Trial* has the bewildering inevitability of a nightmare, punctuated by wild sexual irruptions and queasy conflations of emotions – guilt commingled with impotence, vulnerability with self-belief. The movie switches jarringly between long takes and abrupt cuts, mournful adagios and abrasive jazz. It is the least enjoyable of Welles's films: *you are supposed to have a very unpleasant time. That's the idea.*[215]

Despite his incidental role, Welles establishes himself as storyteller by narrating the opening parable, introducing *a story called The Trial*, post-dubbing almost a dozen characters himself (including the fey artist Titorelli) and, as in *Ambersons*, reading the credits aloud (*I played the Advocate and wrote and directed this film. My name is Orson Welles*). Editing went well but slowly and, despite missing a slot at Venice, Welles was, for the first time, given final cut on a film he didn't produce himself. Opening in Paris that December, the film's portrayal of K came in for criticism from some Kafka purists, though Welles maintained that the character's ambition and selfishness were true to Kafka's text.

Zagreb had offered something besides brutalism: it was there that Orson met and was smitten with Olga Polinkas, daughter of one of the film's designers and a writer and artist (not to mention actor and TV presenter) in her own right. She'd already exhibited sculpture under a pseudonym; Welles was to give her another, Oja Kodar. (In fact Oja was a childhood nickname while 'kodar'

means 'as a gift' in Croatian.) Her intellectual independence and assumption of equal standing were as attractive as her beauty; a mutual friend thought Orson 'very impressed that she doesn't need him to exist.'[216] He returned to Paola and Beatrice in Rome but this new connection would prove equally enduring.

Welles considered his next move — ideas ranged from a

Oja Kodar, pictured some years later

Dostoyevsky movie to a TV *Julius Caesar* to a musical of *Gone with the Wind* – and acted for money. There was more work on *Don Quixote*, which he said was *basically finished. I only need three weeks to film a few things. What worries me is its release . . . everything in the film that was new is now old-fashioned. There are a great deal of jump cuts, fast action shots . . . and they are going to say that I stole it from the Nouvelle Vague and I did it before them.*[217] Welles's relations with the new generation of film-makers were not particularly cordial, despite their admiration. Rather than cultivating the fashionable artists who shared much of his youthful progressivism, he moved the family to Fascist Spain – with which he had 'a secret love affair', as Kodar later put it, 'because Spain was under Franco and it really broke his heart'[218] – and worked on those unreconstructed nostalgists Quixote and Falstaff.

Still trying to realise *Chimes at Midnight*, Welles reached an arrangement with an Italian producer who wanted a *Treasure Island* movie: sure, Orson agreed, he'd make that, but why not have this other picture on the side too? They could even double up on sets and locations. Like *The Trial, Chimes* had an international crew and cast, including Jeanne Moreau as Doll Tearsheet, Margaret Rutherford as Mistress Quickly and John Gielgud as Henry IV. Keith Baxter reprised his stage Hal. Props and costumes were snaffled from the likes of *El Cid* and *The Fall of the Roman Empire* and Welles worked with his usual openness to change, altering the shooting schedule according to the light, weather or actors' moods – 'very larky,' recalled Baxter, 'wonderful.'[219] *Treasure Island* meanwhile received minimal attention; every now and then Welles would hire a boat to get some footage but soon he gave up even this pretence (though he still played Long John Silver in the picture, eventually completed by John Hough). Post-production for *Chimes* took place in Paris and, as usual, dragged on: it took three weeks to edit the battle of Shrewsbury alone. The result was a sequence of astonishing economy, a skirmish whose degeneration from chivalric pomp into squalid, muddy fracas is mirrored by its increasingly violent editing. There were, however, serious problems with the sound processing.

Chimes contains two scenes that may be the best Welles ever acted on screen. The first is the play-acting at the Boar's Head, in which Falstaff and Hal imagine two audiences between Hal and his father, both taking each role in turn. Kingship as a specialised mode of performance was a subject close to Welles's heart. *There used to be a form, a division of actors in France . . . who were called king actors. And I'm a king actor, maybe a bad one, but that's what I am, you see. And I have to play authoritative roles. But Truffaut was quite right when he says about me that I show the fragility of the great authority.*[220] But here Welles does something better than play a fragile king: he plays a fragile king actor, simultaneously expressing the distanced charisma with which he had always been at ease and the neediness behind its operation – comparable in a way to his exposure of Harry Lime. The other scene is Falstaff's climactic ejection

Jeanne Moreau and Welles in *Chimes at Midnight*

from Hal's coronation. The carnival king, ruler of a world turned upside down, cannot hold his position when order is restored; 'being awake,' says Hal, 'I do despise my dream.' Welles's Falstaff visibly deflates; his role as entertainer so abruptly dismissed, he wilts into a fatal resignation more truly sad than the self-pitying bluster of a Kane, Arkadin or Quinlan. His voice and all it stands for have been rejected but Welles's eyes are more heart-breaking here than any words. It is the look of a magician acknowledging how despised he is for his tricks without quite forfeiting his pride in them. As if to emphasise this banishment, Welles gives the closing voice-over narration to another actor; Ralph Richardson's reading from Holinshed's *Chronicles* makes no mention of Falstaff, only of the new king. Posterity, it suggests, has no interest in the fat knight; 'thou'lt forget me when I'm gone', he tells Doll. And yet Falstaff has not been forgotten; we have just watched his story being told.

Shortly after the end of the *Chimes* shoot, Orson turned 50. It is difficult to imagine his response to this landmark. In his youth and as an actor he had always rushed to embrace age. Now that he was 50, he had the inquisitiveness and industry of a young man, even if he had less to show for them than in his heyday. There was, though, to be something of an inward turn in the work of his last two decades, a shift from practising narrative to exploring its operation. He told stories about stories.

The first of these was *The Immortal Story*, which was adapted with unusual fidelity from the story by Isak Dinesen (pen-name of Karen Blixen, one of Welles's favourite writers), although Welles added an opening chorus of local gossips and the death of his character at the end. His first full collaboration with Kodar, it evinced another shift in his work, which he credited to her influence: a fuller engagement with sexuality, shown as a source of pleasure rather than an index of power. As Kodar later said of another of their collaborations, 'you will feel that somebody else worked with him because there are things that he never would have done alone and never did before. He was a very shy man, and erotic stuff was not his thing. And in this film you will see the erotic stuff. He kept accusing me with his finger: "It's your fault!" And he was right – it's my fault!'[221] By now Orson and Oja had established a ménage: he had failed to reply to her letters after leaving Yugoslavia but hearing that she was living in Paris he hired a private detective to track her down and barged into her apartment and life. Paola and Beatrice remained in Madrid, and Welles's devotion to them seems not to have been affected by his new liaison.

Set in Macao, *The Immortal Story* concerns aged millionaire Charlie Clay (Welles), who dislikes fictions. On learning that a report he had heard – of a sailor paid to sleep with a rich merchant's wife – was merely a common nautical fable, he sets about orchestrating its actual occurrence so that at least one young sailor can boast truthfully of such an encounter. Clay pays a woman and a young seaman to enact the tale. At the moment of the lovers' embrace, Clay bursts into their chamber and – unseen, behind a gauze curtain – tells them *you think you move at your own will. Not so. You move at my bidding.* He is like God, the author, the narrator; except that his supposed marionettes determine to keep their time together secret, denying the merchant of his goal. Their refusal compares with Tanya's dismissal of gossip and rumour in *Touch of Evil*, but where that was a mercy, this is a defeat. Like Arkadin, Clay expires with the failure of his story.

The one-hour film was mostly shot near Madrid in autumn 1966. Though it belongs to the tradition of Welles's cinematic rather than television work, it was funded by the French broadcaster RTF, who insisted on colour. Welles was uneasy – *color enhances the set, the scenery, the costumes but mysteriously enough it only detracts from the actors*[222] – but he was partially converted, later saying *I like fog and fire and smoke in color, and winter snow. But it's pretty limited.*[223] *The Immortal Story* was well received when it eventually went out on French TV in May 1968, though the timing can only have emphasised its inwardness. *The Trial, Chimes at Midnight* and *The Immortal Story* are less ingratiating, less keen to chuck you under the chin than his earlier work. He saw only two more films through to fruition and though they would be more personable, they were tricksy, self-reflexive advances of the essay form he had used on TV rather than cinematic narratives. The one conventional story he tried to film was never completed.

At the Cannes premiere of *Chimes* in May 1966 Welles had been asked how he chose his roles. *Money*, he said.[224] And so in the late 60s and early 70s he was in over a dozen films, mostly bad. (One was for his friend John Huston, who had directed *Moby Dick*.) In 1968 he began to collaborate with Peter Bogdanovich on a book of interviews. The young man who had curated the MoMA retrospective seven years earlier was now a director in his own right, soon to make the acclaimed *The Last Picture Show*, and would become a staunch friend and supporter (though their interview book would take 25 years to see print). There was voice-over work on everything from documentaries about the Russian Revolution to *Star Trek* blooper shows. Welles was interviewed for TV and magazines and also – largely thanks to Bogdanovich – became a fixture on US talk shows, often performing Shakespeare or magic tricks (or, on one occasion, receiving a round of applause for applying stage make-up).

In 1967 Orson and Oja began work on a self-funded adaptation of the novel *Dead Calm*, about a couple's sailing holiday interrupted by a maniac (later filmed with Sam Neill and Nicole Kidman). They shot footage for *The Deep*, sometimes called *Dead Reckoning*, in colour off the Dalmatian coast. The extant material is not Welles's most impressive; it is tempting to see the exercise as an excuse for a few weeks on a yacht in the sun, although he continued to attempt to complete the film until 1973. The project seemed to mark a new openness in Welles and Kodar's relationship. They were seen in public together and Paola learned of their affair, but remained remarkably sanguine, apparently reasoning that, as its impact on their family life was minimal and it made Orson happy, there was no need to make a scene. This arrangement – Paola and Beatrice providing domesticity, Oja a stimulating partner and collaborator – persisted until Welles's death.

Welles and Kodar also worked on some Edgar Allen Poe adaptations and, from 1968, a series of comic TV shows known as *Orson's Bag* set in London, Vienna and Venice (where they also shot impressive test scenes, in colour, for a *Merchant of Venice* film). Less travelogues than pegs for comic ideas, the *Orson's Bag* programmes weren't necessarily shot where they were set ('Vienna', for instance, was also Zagreb and Los Angeles) and, though initially funded by CBS, were never screened. The 'London' episode includes a Trafalgar Square monologue, a walkabout in which Orson plays half a dozen stereotypically quaint characters (from a bobby to a flower-seller to a Chinaman) and Orson, his face in shadow, reading from Churchill. There were also Monty Python-like sketches in which he had his girth ridiculed by supercilious tailors, interviewed himself as 'Lord Plumfield' (recording the interviewer cutaways three years later) and played four different codgers in a gentlemen's club. Although he mentions 'Swinging London', the material has more of a post-war feel – Welles, former standard-bearer of liberal progressivism, never really engaged with the social and political upheavals of the 1960s.

It was a busy but scrambled period, in which Welles's constant efforts to realise his own projects rarely succeeded while his profile remained high thanks to roles in other people's films and crowd-pleasing TV appearances. By the end of the decade, Welles was again insisting *Don Quixote* was a hair's breadth from completion. He now had footage of Quixote's misadventures (including an attempt to rescue Paola from the dragon that was her Vespa), Sancho being transfixed by the television and the pair's involvement in a film of *Don Quixote* being made by a director called Orson Welles. There were plans for an expansive autobiographical project, *The One-Man Band*, incorporating interviews with Skipper Hill, and an idea for a TV series about the world's best restaurants. Orson became an increasingly frequent visitor to Hollywood for talk show appearances and movie cameos, including playing conjurors who functioned as father figures in Brian De Palma's debut *Get to Know Your Rabbit* and *A Safe Place* for Henry Jaglom (a wealthy novice director who would become a good friend).

In July 1970 another fan introduced himself, an enthusiastic young cinematographer named Gary Graver just back from serving in Vietnam. He was to be Orson's loyal cameraman for the rest of his life; along with Kodar, they would form a collaborative partnership of a strength and endurance Welles hadn't known since the Mercury. The month after they met, a fire gutted Orson's villa in Madrid in his absence, destroying a substantial personal archive reaching back from recent work through records of *Chimes* on stage and Eartha Kitt in Germany to the *Too Much Johnson* film footage. He took the loss in his stride. It was a perverse gift to a self-mythologiser — at least no one could call him to account on material that no longer existed — and a spur to a new start.

Tearing down the castle 1970–76

*'You may even learn to hate me. Later perhaps that
hatred may wither to the dry husk of admiration.'*

Welles as Mr Delasandro in *Get To Know Your Rabbit*

In June 1966, while based in Spain, Welles had described plans
for a film about a movie director, to be called *Sacred Monsters*.
Rejected by his associates, this Hemingway-Ford-Huston type –
a real *macho [who] can hardly see through the bush of hair on his chest*
– takes to following a matador *who has become in a way his dream of
himself*. The improvised project would take eight weeks at the
most. Following the Madrid fire, Orson relocated more fully to
the US and the idea relocated with him, from Spain and bullfighting to Hollywood and moviemaking. *The Other Side of the
Wind* – as it was now called – centred around veteran director Jake
Hannaford, the film he was struggling to finance after years of
European exile, his 75th birthday party and his death at the
wheel after leaving it. Hannaford's film – also called *The Other Side
of the Wind* – was opportunistically packed with sex, violence
and stylings from the French New Wave. The stronger content
reflected both changed times and the influence of Kodar (who
played Hannaford's female lead).

Rather than eight weeks, Welles would work on the project
for over half a decade – a period in which he received more lavish
praise and stinging opprobrium than at any time since his fall
from grace three decades earlier. Despite the clear parallels

between Hannaford's struggles with backers and backbiters and Orson's own, Welles insisted the film was not autobiographical; determined to ward off such speculation, he declined his obvious casting as the director and began production without a lead. Shooting progressed in the tradition of *Othello* and *Don Quixote* – on and off, when cast and crew could be mustered – in France, California and Arizona (where Orson, Paola and Beatrice lived until 1974; Oja, meanwhile, was installed in the Hollywood Hills). Backing came and went from German TV, a Swiss group and finally the Shah of Iran's brother-in-law; as part of the deal, Welles narrated a grovelling documentary about the despot.

Other projects were under consideration too. The deaths of both leads in *Don Quixote* (Francisco Reiguera, Welles's Don, passed away in 1969 and Akim Tamiroff, his Sancho Panza, three years later) did not stop work on the picture; Welles now viewed it as a more expansive essay on Spain anyway and continued gathering snippets. Graver shot Orson reading short stories at home; Welles and Kodar adapted Conrad and wrote a script about Dumas *père et fils* (Bogdanovich would play Orson's son); Orson was desperate to play Don Corleone in *The Godfather*, the role which eventually went to Marlon Brando, and there was talk of a film with Mick Jagger. He and Graver recorded a Shylock monologue and started an uncompleted one-man variation on *Moby Dick – Rehearsed* in which Welles read excerpts against plain backdrops: the beautiful lighting ranged from moon and water effects to halo-like backlighting, while cross-cutting enabled Welles to converse with himself. Money was as tight as ever: apart from funding *The Other Side of the Wind*, in 1973 the IRS hit Orson with an additional tax bill for $30,000 dating back to 1956. He appeared in magic-themed films like *Necromancy* and *Malpertuis* and on TV as *The Man Who Came to Dinner*, a part based on his old sponsor Alexander Woollcott. He was a guest on *The Dean Martin Show* and *Rowan & Martin's Laugh-In* and guest host for David

Frost and *The Tonight Show*. He introduced silent classics on PBS, mystery shows on British TV and was always doing voice-overs.

Since his days at Todd, Welles seems always to have been juggling a handful of artistic and commercial projects, except when acute depression or nervous exhaustion forced short breaks. Yet it was only the last items on the above list that saw mass distribution, fostering the image of a man trading on his reputation without producing new work to sustain it. In 1970, Charles Higham's *The Films of Orson Welles* – in many ways a sympathetic and perceptive study – argued that the production and editorial problems associated with almost every film since *Kane* were self-inflicted. Welles of course blamed lack of financing, philistinism, treason and his reputation: in 1967 he had complained that *I drag my myth around with me*;[225] and *now*, he sighed, *the legend walks again*.[226]

It was far from all bad. In 1970 Welles was awarded a special Oscar for 'superlative artistry and versatility in the creation of motion pictures' – a belated and somewhat hollow embrace from the industry he had always felt cold-shouldered by. He skipped the ceremony, claiming he was in Spain: *to come out in the middle of all that, with all the lights shining, and try to get a little glisten in the eye and so on – I just thought I'd be crooked to do it*.[227] In 1971 *Kane* again topped *Sight and Sound*'s top ten, which found room for *Ambersons* too. William Friedkin spoke for many younger directors when he said he had been 'inspired to become a film-maker as a direct result of having experienced *Citizen Kane*.'[228] Rarely absent from viewing lists in the growing field of film studies, Welles had a Harvard cinema named after him and politely declined an honorary doctorate from Columbia as depressingly valedictorian. He went out of his way to cultivate sympathetic correspondents from film journals worldwide; like turning the house lights up, it was a way of getting the audience in his corner. The tactic reached its ultimate expression when

Joseph McBride – 25-year-old author of a brilliant 1972 study of Welles's oeuvre – was brought over to *The Other Side* to play a parody of himself at Hannaford's party.

That year also saw the publication of Houseman's memoirs, in which Welles was charismatic, petulant, wonderful and damned; and of an article by the doyenne of the critical establishment Pauline Kael in *The New Yorker* that put Charles Higham's 'fear of completion' theory in the shade. 'Raising *Kane*' claimed that Herman Mankiewicz was, to all intents and purposes, the sole author of *Citizen Kane* and Welles an undeserving credit-stealer. Kael's entertainingly written argument went out of its way to avoid Welles's side of the story or indeed to acknowledge how much a script can be amended and added to during filming. It provoked an argument fought across the pages of various journals, with Bogdanovich, McBride and Jaglom joining Welles in depicting the screenplay as a joint effort. Yet this in itself was an unacknowledged mitigation of the original hype: as ardent an admirer as Kenneth Tynan – who described *Kane* as 'the crucial artistic experience of my life'[229] – was profoundly disillusioned to learn that the film was not the one-man show claimed at the time.

If people had been asking for far too long what Welles had done since *Citizen Kane*, at least he'd done that – along with 'The War of the Worlds' and Harry Lime it remained the basis of his popular artistic persona. Now even that was being challenged (as, indeed, the 'War' script had been). Orson considered suing but was told that his reputation was simply too large: everyone was entitled to an opinion on him, like the White House, the Red Sox or William Randolph Hearst. The bitterest blow was surely the inclusion of 'Raising *Kane*' as the introduction to the published screenplay of *Citizen Kane*: those keen to learn more about this father of cinema – and there were many – were told at the most impressionable stage that he was a fraud. At least he kept his co-author credit.

With his reputation in jeopardy, Welles embarked on a project that offered a sly riposte to his accusers. If they were attacking him for fakery and dubious accreditation, he'd make a film that challenged the very notion of authorship. It started out as a TV essay based on leftover footage from another director's programme: the BBC had recently screened a study of the notorious art forger Elmyr de Hory made by François Reichenbach (maker of an earlier documentary on Welles). Orson, fascinated by credulity and still interested by television as a storytelling medium, saw more potential in his friend's work and was given permission to make use of it. As Orson prepared his take on the material, which included extensive interviews with de Hory and his biographer Clifford Irving, the news broke that Irving himself had pulled the hoax of the decade with his faked autobiography of Howard Hughes. Suddenly the footage acquired several new layers of irony – and potentially profitable topicality – and Welles reimagined it as a feature. Rounding the picture off with the story of Kodar's sojourn as Picasso's muse, he added a third faker: himself. The Picasso story, he cheekily revealed at the end, was bogus; as he said at the beginning, *I'm a charlatan.*

Eventually known as *F for Fake*, this playful documentary was seen as a radical departure, largely because of the low profile of Welles's previous television work. This impression has tended to grow as Orson's TV career becomes ever less well-known, but *F for Fake* has much in common with his earlier factual TV work, and shares some techniques with 'The Fountain of Youth'. As far back as 1958, referring to TV, he had expressed *a passion for films that turn their back on fiction but are nonetheless not of the genre that say, 'Here's the truth, such is life, etc.' Rather, they are made of opinions, the expression of the personality and ideas of the director . . . it's not trying to be factual, it's simply not telling lies. It's in the tradition of a diary, my reflections on any given subject.*[230]

Welles starts with his voice over a black screen, then shows his hands doing close-up magic. 'Up to your old tricks again?' asks Kodar, and the film is full of them. The Hughes affair provides a classic case study of a free-floating reputation, a man of whom people *saw nothing and believed everything they told each other*. We get thoughts on the false pretences that underpinned Orson's debut at the Gate and the 'The War of the Worlds' scare; but the accounts are only half-true. Should we think that Welles has, as Irving says of de Hory, 'developed a fiction about his life and to destroy that fiction would tear down the whole castle . . . The tales he tells now are things that he has built up in his imagination over the years and come to believe as true'? De Hory falls alongside Arkadin and Quinlan, his life's work exposed by a younger investigator, but his forgeries allow for deeper probing into the notions of credit and credibility, authorship and authority. Much is made of the fallibility of the 'experts' who misattributed de Hory's paintings to the greats; are the critics ever worth listening to? Does it matter that Chartres Cathedral lacks a signature? All things pass; *our songs will all be silenced. But what of it? Go on singing. Maybe a man's name doesn't matter*. What does it matter what you say about people?

Orson called the film an expression of his *general revulsion at the whole auteur business*[231] (also evident in *The Other Side of the Wind*). Welles – once so insistent on receiving sole credit for his ventures – now claimed to scoff at the idea of a single motivating genius being responsible for the artistic success of a film. His querying whether the provenance of a work is as important as the pleasure it brings is hardly idle given how much of *F for Fake* is found material. The whole film is a protracted exercise in sleight of hand, even more dependent on editing than *Othello*, and uniquely happy to draw attention to it. *The images alone are insufficient*, Welles once said. *They are very important, but they are only images. The essential thing is how long each image lasts, what follows each image.*

All of the eloquence of a film is created in the editing room.[232] The continual, at times dizzying, conversation of images in *F for Fake* proves that this eloquence can be achieved even with someone else's footage: an insert of de Hory asserting 'that's a fact' at a particularly contentious moment; the suspenseful, utterly fabricated duel of stares between him and Irving; the timely freeze frame, isolating a particularly telling facial expression. The comedy of montage is a great way to redirect attention from the story to its telling, and it was a small leap for Welles to show himself at the editing console. Increasingly he photographed himself in such surroundings. Why bother with facts, he seems to be asking, when I offer you story? *Reality? It's the toothbrush waiting at home for you in its glass, a bus ticket, a paycheck and the grave.*

Welles and camera from *F for Fake*

Welles was childishly excited about the film, hoping to make more like it, but it met with quizzical reviews and poor box office. In July 1974 – shortly before *F for Fake*'s unsuccessful US release – he embarked on a comparable project commissioned by a German TV station. *Filming Othello* offered a kind of attenuated, anecdotal production history of the earlier film, featuring addresses from the Moviola, extensive conversations with Edwards and Mac Liammóir and a question and answer session with a Boston audience. Quoting the Moor, Orson promised he would 'a round, unvarnish'd tale deliver' but the apparently straightforward scenes of Welles conversing with Edwards and Mac Liammóir were as artfully, artificially constructed as anything in *F for Fake*, with Welles' contributions to the 'conversation' recorded weeks, even months later. Even the clips from *Othello* were re-edited, making *Filming Othello* itself as tricksy and unreliable as Iago's tall tales or the original picture's editing.

Welles briefly considered shooting a new epilogue to *Ambersons* with the original actors – hardly the most forward-looking concept – but Holt and Moorehead were dead by 1974. At that time the Welles family moved from Arizona to Las Vegas, partly so Orson could make more frequent appearances on the *Merv Griffin Show*. He was often seen holding forth on politics, magic and, if he must, the old days. The trademark cigar was just for show; now that he weighed in at over 25 stone (159 kg), Orson had followed his doctor's orders and cut down on some of his bad habits.

Meanwhile work still proceeded on *The Other Side of the Wind*. Welles finally cast Hannaford, a full three years into the production, giving the role to John Huston, one of its original models and a friend and collaborator. Orson later described Huston as *a virtuoso actor at being a director*.[233] The film had changed to reflect its creator's changing circumstances: at his party Hannaford now had to fend off hostile critics – proxies for Higham and Kael – as well as negotiating the attentions of documentary-makers, McBride's anal academic and Bogdanovich's alter ego Brooks Otterlake. Orson shot scenes of Hannaford directing sex scenes ('all right, sweetie, you know where to go. Let's have that tongue') and taunting the male star whom he secretly lusted after.

Following *F for Fake* Orson thought he had secured enough funding to complete *The Other Side*, but, he claimed, the middleman pocketed the cash; he and Oja between them eventually spent $750,000 of their own money on the project. The last, best hope of raising funds came in 1975, when the American Film Institute announced Welles was to receive their third Lifetime Achievement Award. Working hard to produce a showreel for the lavish ceremony, Orson planned to challenge the members of the Institute to provide money as well as pay lip service. At the dinner, Welles obligingly roared through every joke made at his expense. Finally called to the stage, Orson – a little croaky, a little wheezy, but still with a steely glint – accepted the honour *in the name of all the mavericks. And also as a tribute to the generosity*

A pat on the back for the maverick: Welles with Frank Sinatra at the AFI tribute

of the rest of you — to the givers — to the ones with fixed addresses. He thanked them and showed a clip from *The Other Side* in which Hannaford's assistant shows a clip from his film to a studio executive. *The stooge,* Welles explained to nervous chuckles, *is trying to sell the unfinished movie that Jake is making and for which he needs end money.* Yet the clip within the clip is wilfully obscure, jolting from black and white to saturated colour, still photos to 'scene missing' signs; the stooge can't explain its weird symbolism, admits there isn't a script and confesses Hannaford has fallen out with the lead. Why on earth, asks the executive, should he consider funding this? The stooge gives a resigned grin: 'he's done it before.'

This was Orson's last demand for love on his own terms; a pitch for a film whose point was proved by its failure to reach completion. Welles received a single offer of funding and rejected it in expectation of a better one that never materialised. There was, he maintained, frustratingly little shooting or even editing left to do but he lacked the cash to see it through and the new chief of his Iranian backers refused further money without being granted final cut. Then the Shah fell, the backers' assets were frozen and the stalemate was left unresolved. It remains so to this day.

When *Filming Othello* was eventually shown in 1978, it ended with Welles making *a confession. This hasn't been as easy as I'd wished. There are too many regrets, too many things I wish I could have done over again. If it wasn't a memory — if it was a project of the future — talking about Othello would have been nothing but delight. Promises are more fun than explanations. With all my heart I wish that I wasn't looking back on Othello but looking forward to it. That* Othello *would be one hell of a picture.* These are the last words of the last film completed by Orson Welles.

The end 1976–85

It would be hard to find a more impressive failure.

From Welles's unfilmed screenplay, *The Big Brass Ring*

A few months after the AFI tribute, Welles moved to Beverly Hills, where he would spend his final decade. It would be the period of his greatest fame since *Kane* and the most barren phase of his professional life. In ten full years not one of his own projects, in any medium, would reach an audience – an unprecedented situation for him. Yet Orson's public persona was everywhere. There were always voice-overs to read and he remained a frequent talk show guest, usually with a conjuring trick to show off. A young magician named Jim Steinmeyer would help Welles prepare; they became good friends. 'None of [the television] people were interested in him doing that stuff,' Steinmeyer maintained. 'I think he didn't have anything to promote and he was really self-conscious about that . . . And so he was there because he had an amazing new illusion to show you . . . of course once he started talking on the panel, that's all anyone really cared about.'[234] For Welles himself magic was more than a fig leaf or hobby. In 1976 he began to develop *The Magic Show*, a feature-length collection of illusions, interviews and anecdotes that he and Gary Graver worked on until his death. Of course, the other person on a talk show who has nothing to plug is the host. Orson had proved himself an excellent listener and interviewer in his earlier TV work and in 1978 and 1979 compiled a talk show pilot. Cameras, monitors and other technical equipment were often featured on screen and the guests included his friend Burt Reynolds and the Muppets (in whose first two movies he had appeared). *It was frankly an attempt to enter the commercial field and earn my living as a talk show master. It was just a flop, that's all, nobody wanted it.*[235]

Welles became sought-after for advertisements, which he preferred to the invariably poor roles he was offered in movies: *I'd rather do an honest commercial than act in a dishonest film.*[236] From 1978 to 1981 Orson starred in a famous campaign for Paul Masson wines; many young people came to know him primarily for the catchphrase *no wine before its time*. Welles saw advertising as another branch of storytelling; one director said 'he goes into commercials like he's thought of the idea. He understands the dynamics of advertising. He respects the craft he's doing. He wants to do the best possible job. He reviews how much the product is selling from the marketing people. I mean, he really goes into this shit.'[237] Has anyone but Welles ever left an advertising gig over creative differences?

Tapes circulated of Orson and the director arguing during a recording session for an advert for Findus frozen foods: 'Can you emphasize a bit "in" – "*in* July"?' asked the director. *Why? That doesn't make any sense! Sorry, there's no known way of saying an English sentence with 'in' and emphasize it! Get me a jury and show me how you can say 'in July' and I'll go down on you! That's just idiotic, if you'll forgive me for saying so.*

Bogdanovich was still planning to publish the interviews carried out from 1969 to 1972; he would send the transcripts to Welles, who would amend and revise them, sometimes concocting whole new exchanges. *Throw it all away, Peter*, he told Bogdanovich of his research, *it can only cripple the fine spirit of invention.*[238] As he told Gore Vidal, *I have made an art form of the interview.*[239]

Then there were the dancing bear lunches at Orson's regular restaurant Ma Maison in Beverly Hills, where he turned on the charm for some young nabob in the hope of securing cash; they usually left in an enchanted daze of promised generosity but later found that, being awake, they despised their dream. Perhaps the most fondly pursued of Orson's putative projects was *The Dreamers*, based on two stories by *The Immortal Story*'s Isak Dinesen, in which an opera singer, Pellegrina Leoni (to be played by Oja), loses her ability to sing, attempts suicide and then sets out in globe-trotting pursuit of as many experiences as possible. 'I will be many persons,' she says. 'All the people in the world ought to be each of them many persons.' Welles was to play her devoted confidant Marcus, permitted to follow her at a distance but not to make contact. He was once again to play a shadow, but this time he would be mute. In the absence of funding, Welles shot some scenes of *The Dreamers* at home on Hollywood Boulevard, starting in 1980. The fragments have been edited into a kind of showreel, which – despite the story's premise – is dominated by the voice of Welles the storyteller.

If *The Dreamers* was a labour of love, Welles followed it with a project specifically conceived as commercial. Henry Jaglom suggested creating a star vehicle that he would try to place with a studio; the result was *The Big Brass Ring*. The lead is Blake Pellarin, the Democrat golden boy who, having just lost a Presidential election, seeks out his old Harvard mentor, Kimball Menaker, now advisor to a central African dictator. Menaker is another of Welles's ambivalent self-portraits, an impressive failure who makes his first appearance, via a tape recorder, as *a rumbling bass-baritone*. The script refers to *Othello* and describes a bestiary like Kane's, a Ferris wheel like Lime's, a carnival like Rio's. Such echoes notwithstanding, it is also Welles's most outward-looking story for years, at least in terms of its political sideswipes. Uniquely among his personal rogue's gallery, Welles let Menaker live. *The Big Brass Ring*, however, did not thrive: Welles secured backing, but it was dependent on signing a major star, none of whom was receptive to the script's mix of politics and homosexuality – not to mention its unsavoury deployment of a plate of eels and a semen-sodden handkerchief.

In a major two-part interview for BBC TV's *Arena* broadcast in May 1982, Orson said of his own short-lived political aspirations: *I didn't think anybody could get elected President who had been divorced and who had been an actor. I made a helluva mistake!*[240] As Welles was writing *The Big Brass Ring* in early 1981, Reagan was settling into his showman administration, exploiting his own brand of intimate rhetoric. Such an approach seemed so much smarter to Orson than that of poor *Dick Nixon*, as Menaker calls him, *mincing about inside his fortress in the Oval Room, all bristling with bugs, hoping a playback would eventually inform him who he really was*[241]; Tricky Dicky as the Hank Quinlan of the White House.

Welles imagined in Presidential mode in Don Simpson's satirical comic *Megaton Man* 1985

When money allowed, work continued on *The Magic Show* and *The Dreamers* and in November 1981 an audience Q&A was filmed in preparation for *Filming 'The Trial'*. It's a very enjoyable encounter but no more than raw material; Welles was never able to shape it at the Moviola editing machine. By now Orson's health, often poor, had become a serious cause for concern. His weight exerted considerable strain on his heart, liver and blood pressure and he often needed a wheelchair or golf cart to get around. His diet was the obvious culprit: a single meal could comprise a bottle of Moët et Chandon followed by *boudin noir aux pommes; terrine de canard* and Porterhouse steak washed down with a Beaujolais; and *mousse à l'Armagnac* with several glasses of Calvados. Welles's doctor placed him on a crash diet: gone were the caviar snacks, the 20 daily coffees, the tumblers of vodka. Confined to fish, fruit and water, Orson fed off his dining companions' enjoyment: *tell me*, he would whisper over a raspberry sherbert or white chocolate mousse, *what are you experiencing at this very moment?*[242]

The award of the Légion d'Honneur in Paris in February 1982 alleviated Welles's ennui. As before, European adoration inspired him afresh and he returned to the idea of a *King Lear* movie. Orson was by now well qualified to embody the king who forfeits his kingdom, demands love on his own terms and pities himself for falling foul of other people's faith in him: 'They told me I was everything,' Lear recalls. ''Tis a lie.' Welles envisaged *not only a new kind of Shakespeare but a new kind of film*[243] dominated by close-ups (for so long the very antithesis of his style); silhouettes would also play a part. He had spoken of his hopes that with the advent of video tape *we can get back to the business of talking directly with the audience, as I did in F for Fake.*[244] *Lear*, he said, would *be done for the small screen, but not as a TV movie. It's cassettes as much as small screens, but it will work in a big theatre.*[245] He shot a six-minute pitch containing his take on the play, which underlined its personal relevance: *the elderly call out for love, for more love than they can possibly receive and for more than they are likely – or capable – of giving back . . . The strong old man, the leader of the tribe . . . demands love as a tyrant demands tribute . . . When, by self-abdication or forced retirement, such a one is suddenly deprived of his own life-sustaining tyranny, he can only flounder to the grave.*[246] No tribute was forthcoming, though Welles continued to look for backers in France.

Welles remained estranged from his two elder daughters: Christopher didn't have his address and his only contact with Rebecca in years was to ask if she'd join him in a commercial. Though Orson was still close to Beatrice, she admitted to finding it hard to reconcile his public persona with the private man who talked about 'the purchase of a new car, weekly household chores, personal goals and problems or the menu for the evening's dinner.'[247]

That other domestic staple TV no longer delighted Orson. *You don't assist television, it's just on . . . Sadat is killed and Lux soap is used and people sit eating food while another soldier bleeds to death in Lebanon and it's unreal.*[248] Nor did he appreciate the opportunity to watch films at home (*I've never cared much for movies, I never cared much for the theater, you, know, I just loved doing it*[249]), let alone his own pictures. *It makes me nervous not being able to change anything,*[250] he explained. *It'd be one long regret.*[251] Once, when friends insisted on watching some of *Ambersons*, he began to cry. Not because of the studio's mutilations; *that just makes me angry. Don't you see? It was because it's the past – it's over.*[252] But it wasn't quite.

In April 1983 Welles was reunited with John Houseman on the *Merv Griffin Show*; it seemed a cordial reconciliation, though there were no further meetings. The following year, however, one of their most famous collaborations suddenly became current again. A producer asked Orson for his approval of a script about the events surrounding Project 891's scandalous 1937 production of *The Cradle Will Rock*. Within weeks, Welles was signed as its producer-director and set about rewriting the story. Straight autobiography had never been Orson's thing. Although willing to furnish embellished anecdotes to Bogdanovich and Barbara Leaming – his official biographer, to whom he would spoon-feed blarney over lunch at Ma Maison – Orson had been obliged to return advances paid for long-overdue memoirs. Here, though, was a chance both to make a picture and to set about his own existence with the genius for editing and reshaping he had brought to so many other subjects. *The way I want to do it is much more interesting than it was!*[253] he declared. Yet, despite making himself the story's focus, Welles avoided self-eulogy. The characterisations of Houseman, Blitzstein and Virginia were generous, while Orson's account of himself was tinged with hubris and self-doubt. The choice to put the play on after the ban was presented as a Faustian bargain: *the people left in it*, 'Orson' acknowledges, *could be punished. It might even turn out that I'm the one who has the most to gain. I could look braver than I am and be more famous than I deserve to be.*[254] While it opened with narration by 'Orson Voice', the film closed with the singers' voices in the darkness and Blitzstein at the piano; Orson had left the theatre.

A decent budget was obtained and pre-production started. Rupert Everett was approached to play young Orson. (Welles would narrate.) Then in November 1984, three weeks before filming was scheduled to start, the financing fell through. Even this enormous knock-back – the collapse of Welles's most personally meaningful and potentially profitable project of the past decade – did not diminish his motivation. He continued developing *The Dreamers* and *The Magic Show*, attempted to secure backing for *Lear*, and tried to navigate the legal quagmire surrounding *The Other Side of the Wind*.

Orson's health, however, continued to deteriorate. By the time he turned 70 in May 1985 his heart was weaker than ever and he had developed diabetes. That summer he started a new script from a story by Oja and engaged an editor for *Don Quixote*. He also played a mentor figure in Henry Jaglom's *Someone to Love* and recited lyrics on a heavy metal track and a soupy single called 'I Know What It Is To Be Young (But You Don't Know What It Is To Be Old)' – a wistful riposte to the presumptuous dressing-up of his 22-year-old self. His most high-profile work comprised voice-overs for the *Transformers* movie and the *Revenge of the Nerds* trailer. On October 9, Welles and Leaming appeared together on the *Merv Griffin Show* and dined at Ma Maison. He went home and sat at his typewriter to plan the next day's shooting for *The Magic Show*. At some point he left a message on Henry Jaglom's answering machine: *This is your friend. Don't forget to tell me how your mother is.*[255] It was the last recording Orson made; the last time he sent his voice out into the darkness. Mothers and magic were on his mind. Early the next morning, his heart failed.

The year before, Orson had recorded a birthday greeting for a friend in which he read from a letter written by the aviator Charles Lindbergh as he approached Paris after crossing the ocean alone: *Within the hour I'll land. And strangely enough, I'm in no hurry to have it pass. I haven't the slightest desire to sleep, there isn't an ache in my body. The night is cool and safe. I want to sit quietly in this cockpit and let the realization of my completed flight sink in. It's like struggling up a mountain after a rare flower and then, when you have it within arm's reach, realizing that happiness and satisfaction lie more in the finding than the plucking. Plucking and withering are inseparable. It's a shame to land with the night so clear and so much fuel in my tanks.*[256] As Welles sat at his desk that cool October night, with so much fuel left unburned in his tanks, did he think of all the flowers he never reached – the unfulfilled works that never blossomed and would never wither? Did he think of a rosebud?

Notes

1 Barbara Leaming, *Orson Welles: A Biography* (Viking, New York: 1985) p 6.
2 Leaming, *Welles*, p 10.
3 Leaming, *Welles*, p 13.
4 Leaming, *Welles*, p 13.
5 Leaming, *Welles*, p 19.
6 Leaming, *Welles*, p 21.
7 Simon Callow, *Orson Welles: The Road to Xanadu* (Jonathan Cape, London: 1995) p 37.
8 Leaming, *Welles*, p 25.
9 Leaming, *Welles*, p 22.
10 Leaming, *Welles*, p 24.
11 Frank Brady, *Citizen Welles* (Scribner, London: 1989) p 12.
12 Brady, *Citizen*, p 11.
13 Callow, *Welles*, p 38.
14 Callow, *Welles*, p 40.
15 Callow, *Welles*, p 48.
16 Callow, *Welles*, p 55.
17 Leaming, *Welles*, p 30.
18 Callow, *Welles*, p 100.
19 Callow, *Welles*, p 94.
20 Callow, *Welles*, p 77.
21 Brady, *Welles*, p 26.
22 Callow, *Welles*, p 85.
23 Callow, *Welles*, p 86.
24 Callow, *Welles*, p 87.
25 Callow, *Welles*, p 102.
26 Booth Tarkington's *Seventeen, Mercury Theatre on the Air*, CBS, 16 October 1938.
27 Orson Welles and Peter Bogdanovich, ed. Jonathan Rosenbaum, *This Is Orson Welles* (HarperCollins, New York: 1992) p 220.
28 Callow, *Welles*, p 117.
29 Callow, *Welles*, p 123.
30 Leaming, *Welles*, p 57.
31 Leaming, *Welles*, p 58.
32 Callow, *Welles*, p 179.
33 Callow, *Welles*, p 141.
34 Callow, *Orson Welles*, p 153.
35 Brady, *Citizen*, p 63.
36 Brady, *Citizen*, p 61.
37 André Bazin, *Orson Welles: A Critical View* (Editions du Cerf, Paris: 1972; Harper & Row, New York: 1978) p 41.
38 Callow, *Welles*, p 188.
39 Leaming, *Welles*, p 79.
40 Callow, *Welles*, p 193.
41 Leaming, *Welles*, p 81.
42 Callow, *Welles*, p 197.
43 Callow, *Welles*, p 207.
44 Bogdanovich, *This Is*, p 12.
45 Leaming, *Welles*, p 110.
46 Callow, *Welles*, p 269.
47 Callow, *Welless*, p 272.
48 Leaming, *Welles*, p 120.
49 Leaming, *Welles*, p 121.
50 Leaming, *Welles*, p 134.
51 David Thomson, Rosebud: *The Story of Orson Welles* (Little Brown, St Ives: 1996) p 79.
52 Leaming, *Welles*, p 137.
53 Thomson, *Rosebud*, p 82.
54 Leaming, *Welles*, p 141.
55 Brady, *Citizen*, p 129.
56 Callow, *Welles*, p 325.
57 Callow, *Welles*, p 340.
58 Herman J Mankiewicz and Orson Welles, *Citizen Kane* (Secker & Warburg, New York: 1971) p 203.
59 Callow, *Welles*, p 337.
60 Brady, *Citizen*, p 126.

61 Callow, *Welles*, p 354.
62 Callow, *Welles*, p 344.
63 Callow, *Welles*, p 356.
64 Callow, *Welles*, p 362.
65 Callow, *Welles*, p 359.
66 Callow, *Welles*, p 373.
67 Callow, *Welles*, p 387.
68 Thomson, *Rosebud*, p 111.
69 Callow, *Welles*, p 413.
70 Callow, *Welles*, p 409.
71 Leaming, *Welles*, p 164.
72 Callow, *Welles*, p 422.
73 *Washington Post* set report, quoted in Brady, *Citizen*, p 191.
74 Callow, *Welles*, p 436.
75 Callow, *Welles*, p 445.
76 Callow, *Welles*, p 444.
77 Introduction to Bazin, *Welles*, p 3.
78 Callow, *Welles*, p 448.
79 Leaming, *Welles*, p 174.
80 Callow, *Welles*, p 461.
81 Thomson, *Rosebud*, p 132.
82 Leaming, *Welles*, p 179.
83 Callow, *Welles*, p 479.
84 Callow, *Welles*, p 478.
85 From 'Raising *Kane*', in Mankiewicz and Welles, *Citizen Kane*, p 54.
86 Brady, *Citizen*, p 244.
87 Monitor, BBC, 13 March 1960 in Mark W Estrin (ed), *Orson Welles. Interviews* (University Press of Mississippi, Mississippi: 1992) p 79.
88 Callow, *Welles*, p 515.
89 Bogdanovich, *This Is*, p 18.
90 Callow, *Welles*, p 531.
91 Brady, *Citizen*, p 284.
92 Callow, *Welles*, p 537.
93 Callow, *Welles*, p 542.
94 Callow, *Welles*, p 551.
95 Callow, *Welles*, p 548.
96 Charles Higham, *Orson Welles: The Rise and Fall of an American Genius* (St Martin's Press, New York: 1985) p 220.
97 Callow, *Welles*, p 567.
98 Callow, *Welles*, p 574.
99 Higham, *Welles*, p 222.
100 *Arena*, BBCTV May 1982 in Estrin, *Interviews* p 185.
101 James Naremore, *The Magic World of Orson Welles* (OUP, Oxford: 1978; revised edition, 1989) p 90.
102 Brady, *Citizen*, p 361.
103 Brady, *Citizen*, p 336.
104 Leaming, *Welles*, p 243.
105 Bogdanovich, *This Is*, p 161.
106 Preface to *The Magnificent Ambersons* in V F Perkins, *The Magnificent Ambersons* (British Film Institute, London: 1999) p 8.
107 Bogdanovich, *This Is*, p 116.
108 Thomson, *Rosebud*, p 219; Higham, Welles, p 247.
109 Leaming, *Welles*, p 244.
110 Higham, *Welles*, p 248.
111 Stefan Drössler (ed), *The Unknown Orson Welles* (Filmmuseum München & Belleville Verlag, Munich: 2004) p 16.
112 Higham, *Welles*, p 254.
113 Brady, *Citizen*, p 347.
114 Welles, *The Big Brass Ring*, p 87.
115 Thomson, *Rosebud*, p 239.
116 Kenneth Williams, *The Kenneth Williams Diaries*, ed Russell Davies (HarperCollins, London: 1993) p 115.
117 Leaming, *Welles*, p 276.
118 Leaming, *Welles*, p 276.
119 Brady, *Citizen*, p 353.
120 Naremore, *Magic World* pp 115-116.
121 Naremore, *Magic World* p 117; Higham, *Welles*, p 268.
122 Brady, *Citizen*, p 375.
123 Bogdanovich, *This Is*, p 185.
124 Leaming, *Welles*, p 298.
125 Leaming, *Welles*, p 300.
126 Leaming, *Welles*, p 299.
127 Brady, *Citizen*, p 378.
128 Bogdanovich, *This Is*, p 385.
129 Brady, *Citizen*, p 379.
130 Bogdanovich, *This Is*, p 174.
131 Brady, *Citizen*, p 380.
132 Higham, *Welles*, p 289.
133 Brady, *Citizen*, p 389.
134 Leaming, *Welles*, p 330.
135 Higham, *Welles*, p 298.
136 Leaming, *Welles*, p 338.
137 Bogdanovich, *This Is*, p 190.

138 Leaming, *Welles*, p 348.
139 Higham, *Welles*, p 310.
140 Brady, *Citizen*, p 413.
141 Bogdanovich, *This Is*, p 219.
142 Bazin, *Welles*, p 30.
143 Brady, *Citizen*, p 431.
144 Leaming, *Welles*, p 360.
145 Brady, *Citizen*, p 435.
146 Thomson, *Rosebud*, p 295.
147 Bogdanovich, *This Is*, p 220.
148 Peter Cowie, *The Cinema of Orson Welles* (A S Barnes, New Jersey: 1973), p 209.
149 Leaming, *Welles*, p 363.
150 Higham, *Welles*, p 317.
151 Leaming, *Welles*, p 370.
152 Brady, *Citizen*, p 440.
153 Brady, *Citizen*, p 437.
154 *Cahiers du Cinéma*, June 1958 in Estrin, *Interviews*, p 40.
155 Leaming, *Orson Welles*, p 377.
156 Leaming, *Welles*, p 381.
157 Leaming, *Welles*, p 383.
158 Higham, *Welles*, p 345.
159 Brady, *Citizen*, p 442.
160 Leaming, *Welles*, p 389.
161 Higham, *Welles*, p 353.
162 Bazin, *Welles* p 100.
163 Higham, *Welles*, p 352.
164 Brady, *Citizen*, p 477.
165 Leaming, *Welles*, p 390.
166 Brady, Citizen, p 478.
167 Leaming, *Welles*, p 392.
168 Brady, *Citizen*, p 471.
169 *Cahiers du Cinéma*, June 1958 in Estrin, *Interviews*, p 40.
170 Leaming, *Welles*, p 394.
171 Brady, *Citizen*, p 469.
172 Brady, *Citizen*, p 472.
173 Leaming, *Welles,* p 397.
174 Bogdanovich, *This Is*, p 3.
175 Brady, *Citizen*, p 484.
176 'The Shadow talks', *New York Times*, 14 August 1938 in Estrin, *Interviews*, p 4.
177 Higham, *Welles*, p 357.
178 Leaming, *Welles*, p 401.
179 Leaming, *Welles*, p 400
180 Leaming, *Welles*, p 400
181 Brady, *Citizen*, p 487.
182 Leaming, *Welles*, p 405.
183 *Filming Othello*.
184 Leaming, *Welles*, p 404.
185 Brady, *Citizen*, p 489.
186 *Cahiers du Cinéma*, June 1958 in Estrin, *Interviews*, p 44.
187 Bogdanovich, *This Is*, p 295.
188 Bogdanovich, *This Is*, p 291.
189 Brady, *Citizen*, p 514; Leaming, *Welles*, p 412.
190 Leaming, *Welles*, p 421.
191 Leaming, *Welles*, p 425.
192 Kenneth Tynan, *Playboy*, March 1967 in Estrin, *Interviews*, p 145.
193 *Monitor*, BBC, 13 March 1960 in Estrin, *Interviews*, p 92.
194 Bogdanovich, *This Is*, p 299.
195 Brady, *Citizen*, p 506.
196 Brady, *Citizen*, p 509.
197 Bogdanovich, *This Is*, p 306.
198 Bogdanovich, *This Is*, p 304.
199 Leaming, *Welles*, p 415.
200 Brady, *Citizen*, p 511.
201 Thomson, *Rosebud*, p 347.
202 Thomson, *Rosebud*, p 356.
203 Leaming, *Welles*, p 457.
204 Leaming, *Welles*, p 440.
205 Brady, *Citizen*, p 519.
206 Bogdanovich, *This Is*, p 294.
207 Estrin, *Interviews*, p 161.
208 Joseph McBride, *Orson Welles* (Secker & Warburg, London: 1972), p 192.
209 Leaming, *Welles*, p 228.
210 Leaming, *Welles*, p 456.
211 Thomson, *Rosebud*, p 368.
212 Thomson, *Rosebud*, p 380.
213 Interview at University of Southern California, 14 November 1981 aka *Filming The Trial*.
214 Bogdanovich, *This Is*, p 247.
215 Bogdanovich, *This Is*, p 284.
216 Leaming, *Welles*, p 459.
217 'Don Quixote' by Esteve Riambau, in Drössler, *Unknown*, p 74.
218 *OW in the land of Don Quixote*.
219 Thomson, *Rosebud*, p 378.
220 *Arena*, BBCTV in Callow, *Welles*, p 319.
221 McBride, *Welles*, p 188.

222 Brady, *Citizen*, p 543.
223 Bogdanovich, *This Is*, p 80.
224 Leaming, *Welles*, p 467.
225 Tynan interview, *Playboy*, March
    1967 in Estrin, *Interviews*, p 136.
226 Bogdanovich, *This Is*, p 151.
227 Leaming, *Welles*, p 511.
228 Brady, *Citizen*, p 553.
229 Kenneth Tynan, *The Diaries of
    Kenneth Tynan*, ed John Lahr
    (Bloomsbury, London: 2001),
    p 358.
230 *Cahiers du Cinéma*, June 1958 in
    Estrin, *Interviews*, p 37.
231 Drössler, *Unknown*, p 64.
232 *Cahiers du Cinéma*, June 1958 in
    Estrin, *Interviews*, p 40.
233 *Arena*, BBCTV, May 1982 in
    Estrin, *Interviews*, p 205.
234 Interview with Peter Tonguette
    in *The Film Journal* 6, 2002,
    www.thefilmjournal.com/issue6/st
    einmeyer.html
235 Drössler, *Unknown*, p 67.
236 Brady, *Citizen*, p 558.
237 Leaming, *Welles*, p 488.
238 Bogdanovich, *This Is*, p 134.
239 *New York Review of Books*, 1 June
    1989 in Estrin, *Interviews*, p 216.
240 *Arena*, BBCTV, May 1982 in
    Estrin, *Interviews*, p 200.
241 Orson Welles and Oja Kodar, *The
    Big Brass Ring* (Black Spring
    Press, California: 1987), p 87.
242 Brady, *Citizen*, p 573.
243 Brady, *Citizen*, p 582.
244 Drössler, *Unknown*, p 56.
245 Drössler, *Unknown*, p 45.
246 Bogdanovich, *This Is*, p 511.
247 Brady, *Citizen*, p 570.
248 Bogdanovich, *This Is*, p 451.
249 Drössler, *Unknown*, p 48.
250 Bogdanovich, *This Is*, p 48.
251 *Filming The Trial*.
252 Bogdanovich, *This Is*, p 132.
253 Leaming, *Welles*, p 514.
254 Orson Welles, *The Cradle Will
    Rock* (Santa Teresa Press,
    California, 1994), p 55.
255 Thomson, *Rosebud*, p 5.
256 Drössler, *Unknown*, p 110.

Chronology

Year	Age	Life
1915		6 May: George Orson Welles born in Kenosha, Wisconsin, to Richard Head Welles and Beatrice Ives Welles. His brother Richard is 10.
1918	3	The Welleses and family friend Dr Maurice 'Dadda' Bernstein move to Chicago.
1919	4	Richard and Beatrice separate.
1924	9	10 May: Beatrice dies from hepatitis, aged 43.
1926	11	Orson joins the Todd School in Woodstock, Illinois, where he produces, directs and stars in a number of stage plays. Headmaster Roger 'Skipper' Hill will remain a lifelong friend.
1930	15	Travels to China and Japan with his father, who dies from alcohol-related illness on December 28 aged 58.
1931	16	Tours Ireland and, in September, joins Dublin's Gate Theatre. 13 October: professional debut as Duke Karl Alexander in *Jew Süss*.

Chronology

Year	History	Culture
1915	Dardanelles/Gallipoli campaign (until 1916). Italy denounces its Triple Alliance with Germany and Austria-Hungary.	Twelve-reel *Birth of a Nation*, first modern motion picture, grosses $18m. Picasso, *Harlequin*.
1918	In Russia, Tsar Nicholas II and family executed. 11 November: Armistice agreement ends First World War.	Amédée Ozenfant and Le Corbusier, *Après le Cubisme*. Paul Klee, *Gartenplan*.
1919	Treaty of Versailles: formal end of First World War. In US, prohibition begins.	Charlie Chaplin, Douglas Fairbanks, D W Griffith and Mary Pickford form United Artists.
1924	Vladimir Lenin dies.	Forster, *A Passage to India*.
1926	Germany joins League of Nations. Hirohito becomes emperor of Japan.	Hemingway, *The Sun Also Rises*. A A Milne, *Winnie the Pooh*. Fritz Lang, *Metropolis*.
1930	Mahatma Gandhi leads Salt March in India. Frank Whittle patents turbo-jet engine. Pluto discovered.	The Hays Office institutes the Production Code guide lines of moral standards in the movies.
1931	King Alfonso XIII flees; Spanish republic formed. Building of Empire State Building completed in New York.	St-Exupéry, *Vol de nuit*. *City Lights* (starring Charlie Chaplin).

Year	Age	Life
1933	18	Recruited to Guthrie McClintic and Katherine Cornell's theatre company for tour of *Romeo and Juliet, The Barretts of Wimpole Street* and *Candida*.
1934	19	Publication of *Everybody's Shakespeare*. OW orchestrates Todd summer drama school and festival, where he meets Virginia Nicolson. 14 November: Virginia and OW marry. *Romeo and Juliet* reaches New York, where OW gets his first radio work.
1935	20	Meets John Houseman. Plays lead in *Panic* on Broadway. Radio work continues.
1936	21	14 April: OW and Houseman's 'voodoo' *Macbeth* opens in Harlem. September 26: *Horse Eats Hat*, the first production of OW and Houseman's federally-funded Project 891 theatre company, opens.
1937	22	January 8: Project 891's *Doctor Faustus* opens to great acclaim. Radio work continues with *Les Misérables*, the first series on which OW has creative control, and the lead role in *The Shadow*. 16 June: 891's 'workers' opera' *The Cradle Will Rock* opens despite orders to suspend all federal productions. OW and Houseman form the independent Mercury Theatre. 11 November: Mercury's *Julius Caesar* opens triumphantly.
1938	23	27 March: OW and Virginia's daughter Christopher is born. 29 April: Mercury's *Heartbreak House* opens. 9 May: OW appears on cover of *Time* magazine. 11 July: *The Mercury Theatre on the Air – First Person Singular*, a series of radio dramatisations of classic literature, begins on CBS. 30 October: *The Mercury Theatre* on the Air's production of 'The War of the Worlds' causes a national scare. 2 November: The Mercury's *Danton's Death* opens.
1939	24	20 July: OW and the Mercury company arrive in Hollywood; he signs a two-picture deal as producer-director-writer-star for RKO pictures.

Year	History	Culture
1933	Adolf Hitler appointed German chancellor. F D Roosevelt president in US; launches New Deal.	Gertrude Stein, *The Autobiography of Alice B Toklas*.
1934	In China, Mao Tse Tung starts on the Long March. Enrico Fermi sets off first controlled nuclear reaction.	Agatha Christie, *Murder on the Orient Express*. Henry Miller, *Tropic of Cancer*.
1935	In Germany, Nuremberg Laws enacted. Philippines becomes self-governing. Italy invades Ethiopia.	George Gershwin, *Porgy and Bess*. Marx Brothers, *A Night at the Opera*.
1936	Germany occupies Rhineland. Edward VIII abdicates throne in Britain; George VI becomes king. Spanish Civil War (until 1939).	RCA experiments with television broadcasts from the Empire State Building.
1937	Japan invades China: Nanjing massacre. Arab-Jewish conflict in Palestine.	Jean-Paul Sartre, *La Nausée*. John Steinbeck, *Of Mice and Men*. Picasso, *Guernica*.
1938	Kristallnacht: in Germany, Jewish houses, synagogues and schools are burnt down, and shops looted.	Warner Brothers produce *Confessions of a Nazi Spy*, although Germany represents 30% of the profits.
1939	1 September: Germany invades Poland. Francisco Franco becomes dictator of Spain. Britain and France declare war on Germany.	Steinbeck, *The Grapes of Wrath*. David O Selznick, *Gone with the Wind*.

Year	Age	Life
1940	25	OW and Virginia divorce in February. 16 July: Script for *Citizen Kane* is finished. Shooting starts on 22 July and is finished by 23 October.
1941	26	Scandal over *Citizen Kane*'s supposed use of William Randolph Hearst's life. Enormous pressure on RKO to suppress the picture. 24 March: *Native Son*, directed by OW for Houseman, opens on Broadway. 1 May: *Citizen Kane* opens to ecstatic reviews but disappointing box office. 28 October: Shooting begins on *The Magnificent Ambersons*, concluding on 31 January.
1942	27	2 February: OW leaves for Brazil to shoot *It's All True*. July 10: *The Magnificent Ambersons* is released without promotion. 22 August: OW returns to the US.
1943	28	3 August: *The Mercury Wonder Show* opens in Hollywood. 7 September: OW and Rita Hayworth marry. October: OW's first editorials in the *New York Post* and *Free World* magazine.
1944	29	*Orson Welles Almanac* begins broadcasting weekly on CBS radio in January. 1 September: OW delivers the first of many speeches in support of FD Roosevelt's re-election campaign. 7 December: OW and Rita's daughter Rebecca is born. The radio series *This Is My Best* begins.
1945	30	22 January: OW begins a regular column in the *New York Post*. OW also undertakes a national lecture tour on fascism. 16 September: *Orson Welles Commentaries* on social and political affairs begins on ABC radio. 21 November: Shooting completed on *The Stranger*.

Year	History	Culture
1940	Germany occupies France, Belgium, the Netherlands, Norway and Denmark. In Britain, Winston Churchill becomes PM. Leon Trotsky assassinated in Mexico.	Ernest Hemingway, *For Whom the Bell Tolls*. Chaplin, *The Great Dictator*.
1941	Germany invades Soviet Union. Japan attacks Pearl Harbour: US enter Second World War. In US, Manhattan Project begins.	Fitzgerald's Hollywood novel, *The Last Tycoon*, is published posthumously.
1942	World's first nuclear reactor constructed at the University of Chicago. German Sixth Army encircled in Stalingrad; Erwin Rommel defeated at El Alamein.	Frank Sinatra makes stage debut in New York. *Casablanca* (starring Ingrid Bergman and Humphrey Bogart).
1943	Allies bomb Germany. Allies invade Italy: Mussolini deposed. Albert Hoffman discovers hallucinogenic properties of LSD.	Rodgers and Hammerstein, *Oklahoma*. Sartre, *Being and Nothingness*. T S Eliot, *Four Quartets*.
1944	Allies land in Normandy: Paris is liberated. Civil war in Greece.	Adorno and Horkheimer's essay on the 'Culture Industry'
1945	8 May: Germany surrenders. United Nations formed. F D Roosevelt dies; Harry Truman becomes US president. Atomic bombs dropped on Hiroshima and Nagasaki.	Benjamin Britten, *Peter Grimes*. George Orwell, *Animal Farm*. Karl Popper, *The Open Society and Its Enemies*. UNESCO founded.

Year	Age	Life
1946	31	31 May: OW's mammoth Broadway musical based on *Around the World in 80 Days* opens. 2 July: *The Stranger* is released. 28 July: OW relates the case of Isaac Woodward, Jr, a decorated black army veteran beaten blind by South Carolina law enforcement, on his *Commentaries* show. The *Commentaries* end in October.
1947	32	28 May: OW directs *Macbeth* for the Utah Centennial Festival, Salt Lake City, shooting a film based on the production from 23 June to 17 July, after which he leaves for Italy. 11 November: OW and Rita Hayworth divorce.
1948	33	30 May: *The Lady from Shanghai* is released. 1 October: *Macbeth* released. That autumn OW also begins work on his film of *Othello*.
1949	34	April: *The Third Man* is released. Work on *Othello* continues, funded largely by OW's roles in other films.
1950	35	15 June: *The Blessed and the Damned*, a presentation of two short plays, is well received in Paris. A variation, *An Evening with Orson Welles*, tours Germany.
1951	36	*The Lives of Harry Lime* is broadcast on BBC radio. 1 October: OW directs and stars in *Othello* in London's West End.
1952	37	The film of *Othello* is premiered at the Cannes Film Festival in May, where it wins the Palme d'Or.

Year	History	Culture
1946	In Argentina, Juan Perón becomes president. In India, Bombay legally removes discrimination against "untouchables". Churchill makes 'Iron Curtain' speech.	Bertrand Russell, *History of Western Philosophy*. Sartre, *Existentialism and Humanism*. Eugene O'Neill, *The Iceman Cometh*.
1947	Truman Doctrine: US promises aid to countries threatened by Soviet expansion plans. India becomes independent. Chuck Yeager breaks the sounds barrier.	Tennessee Williams, *A Streetcar named Desire*. Albert Camus, *The Plague*. Anne Frank, *The Diary of Anne Frank*.
1948	Marshall plan (until 1951). Berlin crisis and airlift. In South Africa, Apartheid legislation passed. Gandhi is assassinated. State of Israel founded.	Brecht, *The Caucasian Chalk Circle*. Greene, *The Heart of the Matter*. Norman Mailer, *The Naked and the Dead*.
1949	NATO formed. Republic of Ireland formed. Mao proclaims China a People's Republic.	George Orwell, *1984*. Simone de Beauvoir, *The Second Sex*. Arthur Miller, *Death of a Salesman*.
1950	Schuman Plan. Korean War begins. Stereophonic sound invented. First successful kidney transplant.	In US, McCarthyism starts (to 1954). Billy Wilder, *Sunset Boulevard*.
1951	Anzus pact in Pacific.	J D Salinger, The Catcher in the Rye.
1952	Nasser leads coup in Egypt. McCarthy era begins in US.	Hemingway, *The Old Man and the Sea*. Samuel Beckett, *Waiting for Godot*.

Year	Age	Life
1953	38	7 September: *The Lady in the Ice*, a ballet for which OW wrote the libretto and designed the sets, opens in Paris. 18 October: Briefly returns to US to star in *King Lear*, directed by Peter Brook for CBS TV's *Omnibus*.
1954	39	Shooting on *Mr Arkadin*; OW loses editorial control after missing a Christmas deadline. Also takes roles in other films.
1955	40	March: *Mr Arkadin* released. It is later released in the UK as *Confidential Report*. 24 April: The six-part *Orson Welles' Sketch Book* begins a successful weekly run on BBC TV. 8 May: OW and Paola Mori marry. 16 June: *Moby Dick – Rehearsed* staged in the West End. Over summer OW makes *Around the World with Orson Welles*, a series of six travelogues broadcast on ITV. October: OW returns to New York to direct and star in *King Lear* on stage. 13 November: OW and Paola's daughter Beatrice born in New York.
1956	41	12 January: *King Lear* opens to mixed reviews and soon closes after OW breaks both ankles and performs from a wheelchair. In spring OW performs in Las Vegas. 8-11 May: OW films 'The Fountain of Youth', pilot for a TV series which is never picked up. OW works on ideas for other TV projects.
1957	42	OW signs on with Universal to re-write and direct *Badge of Evil* (later renamed *Touch of Evil*) with Charlton Heston, as well as play its villain.
1958	43	OW films an interview with Gina Lollobrigida for ABC; it is never aired. 8 June: *Touch of Evil* wins the grand prize at the Brussels World's Fair Film Festival.

Year	History	Culture
1953	Stalin dies. Eisenhower becomes US president. Korean War ends. Francis Crick and James Watson discover double helix (DNA).	Dylan Thomas, *Under Milk Wood*. Arthur Miller, *The Crucible*. *I Vitelloni*.
1954	Insurrection in Algeria. French withdrawal from Indochina: Ho Chi Minh forms government in North Vietnam.	Kingsley Amis, *Lucky Jim*. J R R Tolkien, *The Lord of the Rings*. Bill Haley and the Comets, '*Rock Around the Clock*'.
1955	West Germany joins NATO. Warsaw Pact formed.	Tennessee Williams, *Cat on a Hot Tin Roof*. Vladimir Nabokov, *Lolita*.
1956	Nikita Khruschev denounces Stalin. Suez Crisis. Revolts in Poland and Hungary. Fidel Castro and Ernesto 'Che' Guevara land in Cuba. Transatlantic telephone service links US to UK.	Lerner (lyrics) and Loewe (music), *My Fair Lady*. Elvis Presley, '*Heartbreak Hotel*', '*Hound Dog*', '*Love Me Tender*'. John Osborne, *Look Back in Anger*.
1957	Treaty of Rome: EEC formed. USSR launches Sputnik 1. Ghana becomes independent.	The Academy excludes anyone on the Hollywood blacklist from consideration for Oscars (to 1959).
1958	Great Leap Forward launched in China (until 1960). Castro leads communist revolution in Cuba.	Boris Pasternak, *Dr Zhivago*. Claude Lévi-Strauss, *Structural Anthropology*.

Year	Age	Life
1959	44	At the Cannes film festival in May, OW, Dean Stockwell and Bradford Dillman share the best actor award for their work in Richard Fleischer's *Compulsion*. Over the next 18 months OW appears in more films and shoots on *Don Quixote*.
1960	45	13 February: *Chimes at Midnight* is staged at the Dublin Gate Theatre. 28 April: Ionesco's *Rhinoceros*, directed by OW and starring Laurence Olivier and Joan Plowright, opens at London's Royal Court Theatre.
1961	46	Most of the year is spent planning *The Trial* and making the travelogue series *Nella Terra di Don Chisiotte*, broadcast on Italian TV in from December 1964.
1962	47	While shooting *The Trial* in Paris and Zagreb OW meets Olga Palinkas, aka Oja Kodar, his companion and collaborator throughout his later life. 5 June: Shooting finishes. 21 December: *The Trial* released.
1964	49	Shooting starts on *Chimes at Midnight* and is completed the following April.
1966	51	8 May: *Chimes at Midnight* released, in some regions under the title *Falstaff*. September to November: Shooting on *The Immortal Story* in Paris and Madrid. December: *A Man for All Seasons*, in which OW plays Cardinal Wolsey, is released.
1967	52	OW and Oja Kodar personally finance shooting on the unfinished film *The Deep* off the Dalmatian coast.

Year	History	Culture
1959	In US, Alaska and Hawaii are admitted to the union. Solomon Bandaranaike, PM of Ceylon (Sri Lanka), is assassinated.	In Detroit, Berry Gordy founds Motown Records. *Ben Hur* (dir. William Wyler). Günter Grass, *The Tin Drum*.
1960	Vietnam War begins (until 1975). OPEC formed. Oral contraceptives marketed.	Fellini, *La Dolce Vita*. Alfred Hitchcock, *Psycho*.
1961	Berlin Wall erected. Bay of Pigs invasion. Yuri Gagarin is first man in space	The Rolling Stones are formed. Rudolf Nureyev defects from USSR.
1962	Cuban missile crisis. Satellite television launched.	Edward Albee, *Who's Afraid of Virginia Woolf?* David Lean, Lawrence of Arabia.
1964	Khruschev ousted by Brezhnev. Civil Rights Act in US. PLO formed. Word processor invented.	Bock (music) *Fiddler on the Roof*. Stanley Kubrick, *Doctor Strangelove*.
1966	Indira Gandhi becomes prime minister of India. In China 'Cultural Revolution'. Ian Smith declares Rhodesia a republic.	Avant-garde rock band the Velvet Underground does multi-media shows with Pop artist Andy Warhol.
1967	Military coup in Athens. Six Day War between Israel and the Arab States. Martin Luther King launches a campaign of civil disobedience.	Warhol, *Marilyn Monroe*. *Hair* (musical) opens in New York. The Beatles, *Seargeant Pepper's Lonely Hearts Club Band*. The Doors, *The Doors*.

Year	Age	Life
1968	53	24 May: *The Immortal Story* released in French cinemas and shown on French TV. Filming on *Orson's Bag*, an unfinished TV project, and an unreleased *Merchant of Venice* project.
1970	55	OW given a special Academy Award for 'superlative artistry and versatility in the creation of motion pictures'. August: fire at OW's house in Madrid destroys many possessions, including a substantial work archive. OW begins shooting *The Other Side of the Wind*, working on it for the next six years but never completing the film.
1971	56	Pauline Kael's article 'Raising *Kane*' questions OW's co-authorship of *Citizen Kane*.
1972	57	the OW begins work on film eventually known as *F for Fake*, which is completed the following summer.
1974	59	July: *Filming 'Othello'* begins shooting in Paris. September: *F for Fake* premieres.
1975	60	February: OW receives the American Film Institute's third Life Achievement Award in Los Angeles and relocates to Beverly Hills.
1976	61	OW largely completes filming on *The Other Side of the Wind* and begins shooting the unfinished *The Magic Show*, on which he continues working until his death.
1978	63	OW works on unfinished projects including an autobiographical feature and a TV talk show.

Year	History	Culture
1968	Tet Offensive. In US, M L King and Robert Kennedy assassinated. In Paris, student riots.	Kubrick, 2001: *A Space Odyssey*. The Rolling Stones, *Beggar's Banquet*.
1970	First-ever meeting of East and West German heads of government. In Cambodia: Prince Sihanouk is overthrown, US troops withdraw and Khmer Rouge takes over.	Simon and Garfunkel, *Bridge Over Troubled Water*. The Beatles officially split up. Death from drug overdose of guitarist Jimi Hendrix.
1971	In Uganda, Idi Amin seizes power. Nixon proclaims end of US offensive role in Vietnam War.	Dmitri Shostakovich, *Symphony No. 15*. Kubrick, *A Clockwork Orange*.
1972	In US, Watergate scandal. Bloody Sunday massacre (N Ireland). Allende overthrown in Chile; Pinochet takes power.	Richard Adams, *Watership Down*. Bertolucci, *Last Tango in Paris*. Francis Ford Coppola, *The Godfather*.
1974	West German chancellor Willy Brandt resigns. Turkey invades Cyprus. In the US: Presidents Nixon admits complicity in Watergate cover-up and resigns.	Solzhenitsyn is expelled from the USSR after publication of *The Gulag Archipelago*.
1975	Civil war in Lebanon. Last US personnel flee Saigon by helicopter.	Queen, *Bohemian Rhapsody* (first rock video). Primo Levi, *The Periodic Table*.
1976	Chairman Mao dies. Soweto massacre.	Alex Haley, *Roots*.
1978	Pope John Paul II elected. Camp David Accord. First test-tube baby born.	John Irving, *The World According to Garp*. Michael Cimino, *The Deer Hunter*.

Year	Age	Life
1979	64	*Filming Othello* is shown on German TV.
1980	65	Filming on the unfinished *The Dreamers* begins.
1981	66	OW and Oja Kodar begin writing a political thriller, *The Big Brass Ring*, which does not find backing.
1982	67	23 February: OW awarded the Légion d'Honneur in Paris. Begins searching for funding for a *King Lear* film.
1984	69	OW makes extensive plans for a film, which he will direct and narrate, based on the 1937 production of *The Cradle Will Rock*. Financing collapses shortly before production is scheduled to begin.
1985	70	OW continues working on *King Lear*, *The Magic Show* and *The Dreamers*. 10 October: After appearing on a talk show the night before, OW dies of heart failure at his home in Hollywood.

Year	History	Culture
1979	In UK, Thatcher becomes PM.	Woody Allen, *Manhattan*.
1980	In US, Reagan elected president.	Spielberg, *ET*.
1981	Greece enters the EC. Iran releases US hostages.	Lloyd Webber, *Cats* (musical), based on poems by T S Eliot.
1982	Falklands conflict between United Kingdom and Argentina. In Poland: Solidarity demonstrations.	
1984	Indian troops storm Sikh Golden Temple at Amritsar: Indira Gandhi assassinated by her Sikh bodyguard.	The Band Aid single *'Do They Know It's Christmas?'* raises £8 million for famine relief in Africa.
1985	Gorbachev calls for glasnost ('openness') in Soviet life and a policy of perestroika ('reconstruction').	Norman Foster: HSBC building, Hong Kong. Richard Rogers: Lloyds of London.

List of Works

NB Welles adapted or edited almost all productions from texts by other writers. Most appearances in other directors' films not listed.

THEATRE

1931   *Jew Süss* (act), Gate Theatre, Dublin, followed by other roles.

1934   *Trilby* (dir, act), Todd Theatre Festival.
       Romeo & Juliet, *Candida*, *The Barretts of Wimpole Street* (act), east coast tour.

1935   *Panic* (act), Imperial Theatre, New York.

1936   *Macbeth* (dir), Negro Theatre Unit, Lafayette Theatre, Harlem, New York.
       Horse Eats Hat (dir, wr, act), Project 891, Maxine Elliot Theatre, New York, with Joseph Cotten.

1937   *Doctor Faustus* (dir, act), Project 891.
       The Cradle Will Rock (dir), Project 891, Venice Theatre, New York.
       Julius Caesar (dir, act), Mercury Theatre, New York.

1938   *The Shoemaker's Holiday* (dir), Mercury.
       Heartbreak House (dir, act), Mercury.
       Too Much Johnson (dir, act), Mercury, east coast tour (ends before reaching New York). Includes 40 minutes of filmed material.
       Danton's Death (dir, act), Mercury.

1939   *Five Kings* (dir, act), Mercury, with Burgess Meredith, east coast tour (ends before reaching New York).
       The Green Goddess (dir, act), plays on RKO Vaudeville circuit.

1941   *Native Son* (dir), Mercury, St James Theater, New York.

1943   *The Mercury Wonder Show* (prod, dir, act), circus tent on Cahuenga Boulevard, Los Angeles.

1946   *Around the World in 80 Days* (dir, act), with songs by Cole Porter.

1947   *Macbeth* (dir, act) for Utah Centennial Festival, Salt Lake City, Utah.

1950   *The Blessed and the Damned* (dir, wr, act), Théâtre Edouard VII, Paris, with Eartha Kitt.

1951   *Othello* (dir, act), St James's Theatre, London.

1953   *The Lady in the Ice* (wr, design), Ballet de Paris, Stoll Theatre, London.

1955   *Moby Dick* – Rehearsed (dir, wr, act), Duke of York's Theatre, London.
1956   *King Lear* (dir, act), City Center, New York.
1960   *Chimes at Midnight* (dir, act), Grand Opera House, Belfast, Dublin.
        Rhinoceros (dir), Royal Court Theatre, London, with Laurence Olivier.

R A D I O
1937   *Les Misérables* (dir, act), Mutual radio network.
        The Shadow (act), CBS radio network. Ends 1939.
1938   *The Mercury Theatre on the Air – First Person Singular* (prod, dir, act). 'War
        of the Worlds' broadcast October 1938.

F I L M
1934   *The Hearts of Age* (dir, wr, act), 10-minute film.
1938   *Too Much Johnson* (dir, act), Mercury. With Joseph Cotten, east coast tour
        (ends before reaching New York). Includes 40 minutes of filmed material.
1939   *Heart of Darkness* (dir, act), Mercury/RKO. Plans for film adaptation
        come to nothing.
1941   *Citizen Kane* (prod, dir, co-wr, act), 119 minutes, with Joseph Cotten,
        George Coulouris, Agnes Moorehead, Everett Sloane, Ray Collins.
        Music by Bernard Herrmann.
1942   *The Magnificent Ambersons* (prod, dir, v/o), 88 minutes, with Joseph
        Cotten, Agnes Moorehead, Ray Collins.
        It's All True (prod, dir, wr). Location shooting in Brazil and Mexico
        (under Norman Foster), never completed.
1943   *Journey Into Fear* (prod, co-wr, act), 69 mins, dir Norman Foster, with
        Joseph Cotten, Everett Sloane, Dolores del Rio.
        Jane Eyre (act), 96 mins, dir Robert Stevenson.
1946   *The Stranger* (dir, act), 95 mins, with Edward G Robinson.
1948   *The Lady from Shanghai* (dir, act), 86 mins, with Rita Hayworth, Everett
        Sloane.
        Macbeth (dir, act), 107 mins.
1949   *The Third Man* (act), 93 mins, dir Carol Reed, with Joseph Cotten.
1952   *Othello* (dir, act), 91 mins, with Micheál Mac Liammóir.
1955   *Mr Arkadin* (dir, wr, act), 100 mins, with Akim Tamiroff. US release
        1962.
        Don Quixote (prod, dir, wr, act), work on uncompleted film continues for
        decades.
1958   *Touch of Evil* (dir, wr, act), 93 mins, with Charlton Heston, Janet Leigh,
        Akim Tamiroff, Marlene Dietrich and a cameo by Joseph Cotton.
1959   *Compulsion* (act), 103 mins, dir Richard Fleischer.
1962   *The Trial* (dir, act), 118 mins, with Anthony Perkins, Akim Tamiroff
        and Jeanne Moreau.

1966   *Chimes at Midnight* (dir, act), 119 mins, with John Gielgud, Ralph
        Richardson and Jeanne Moreau.
        A Man for All Seasons (act), 116 mins, dir Fred Zinnemann.
1967   *The Deep aka Dead Reckoning* (prod, dir, act), shooting on uncompleted
        film with Oja Kodar.
1968   *The Immortal Story* (dir, act), 58 mins, with Jeanne Moreau. Simultaneous
        release in cinemas and on French TV.
1970   *The Other Side of the Wind* (prod, dir, wr, act), work on uncompleted film
        with John Huston and Oja Kodar continues for almost a decade.
1974   *F for Fake* (dir, co-wr, act), 85 mins, with Oja Kodar.
1976   *The Magic Show* (prod, dir, wr, act), work on uncompleted film continues
        until death.
1979   *Filming Othello* (dir, wr, act), 90 mins, shown on German TV.
1980   *The Dreamers* (prod, dir, act), work with Oja Kodar on uncompleted film
        continues until death.
1981   *The Big Brass Ring* (co-wr), screenplay written with Oja Kodar fails to
        find backing.
1984   *The Cradle Will Rock* (dir, wr, v/o), film about Welles's 1937 stage pro-
        duction loses backing at last minute.

TELEVISION

1953   *King Lear* (act), CBS TV.
1955   *Orson Welles Sketchbook* (wr, act), BBC TV.
        Around the World with Orson Welles (dir, wr, act), Associated
        Rediffusion/ITV TV.
1956   'Fountain of Youth' (dir, wr, act), pilot for TV show that is never picked up.
1958   *Portrait of Gina* (dir, wr, act), ABC TV, never aired.
1961   *Nella Terra di Don Chisotte* (dir, wr, act), RAI TV.
1968   *The Immortal Story* (dir, act), 58 mins, with Jeanne Moreau. Simultaneous
        release in cinemas and on French TV.
1979   *Filming Othello* (dir, wr, act), 90 mins, shown on German TV.

Since his death, Orson Welles has featured as a character in a number of films.
In *Heavenly Creatures* (Peter Jackson, 1994) he appears in animated fantasy
sequences as a bulbous, grotesque bogeyman, while in *Ed Wood* (Tim Burton,
1994) the radiantly lit Vincent D'Onofrio played him as a role model for that
film's wannabe auteur. In *RKO 281* (1999), about the making of *Citizen Kane*,
Liev Schreiber's Welles was a heroic, uncompromising visionary; in *Cradle Will
Rock*, Tim Robbins's account of the controversial FTP production (1999, not
based on Welles's script), Angus MacFadyen's Orson is an egotistical smooth
operator constantly bickering with Cary Elwes's prissy John Houseman.

Further Reading

Bazin, André, *Orson Welles: A Critical View* (Editions du Cerf, Paris: 1972; Harper & Row, New York: 1978): typically pithy, insightful survey of OW's films from *Citizen Kane* to *Touch of Evil*, with contributions from François Truffaut and Jean Cocteau.

Berg, Chuck and Tom Erskine, *The Encyclopedia of Orson Welles* (Checkmark Books, New York: 2003): generally reliable on the major works but has a large number of omissions, especially from among OW's minor and unfinished projects.

Brady, Frank, *Citizen Welles* (Scribner's, London: 1989): sympathetic biography with excellent detail on less well-known work.

Callow, Simon, *Orson Welles: The Road to Xanadu* (Jonathan Cape, London: 1995): meticulously researched and eloquently argued biography of OW's life up to *Citizen Kane*; the early part of the present book is much indebted to this, though its detail might prove over-thorough for some.

Carringer, Robert L, *The Making of Citizen Kane* (UCP, California: 1985): comprehensive account of the production history of OW's first feature.

Conrad, Peter, *Orson Welles: The Stories of His Life* (Faber and Faber, London: 2003): collection of clever biographical essays presenting OW in the context of a series of personae with whom Conrad argues OW evinced an affinity.

Cowie, Peter, *The Cinema of Orson Welles* (A S Barnes, New Jersey: 1973): one of the first and best studies of OW's film career.

Drazin, Charles, *In Search of The Third Man* (Methuen, London: 1999): well-researched production history.

Drössler, Stefan (ed), *The Unknown Orson Welles* (Filmmuseum München & Belleville Verlag, Munich: 2004): essential collection of articles, interviews, stills and illustrations relating to OW's less familiar and incomplete work.

Estrin, Mark W (ed), *Orson Welles Interviews* (University Press of Mississippi, Mississippi: 1992): invaluable collection of OW interviews ranging from publicity for *The Shadow* in 1938 through his arrival in Hollywood, conversations with *Cahiers du Cinéma* and the BBC's Huw Weldon to the *Playboy* interview with Kenneth Tynan and *Arena* profile in 1982.

France, Richard, *The Theatre of Orson Welles* (Bucknell University Press,

Pennsylvania: 1977): probably the best volume on OW's stage work, benefiting from extensive research and contextualisation.

Higham, Charles, *Orson Welles: The Rise and Fall of an American Genius* (St Martin's Press, New York: 1985): biography by the author whose 'fear of completion' theory dogged OW's latter years, about which the book has far less detail than it does about his ancestors.

Houseman, John, *Run-Through* (Simon & Schuster, New York: 1972): memoirs dealing with Houseman's theatrical collaborations with OW, this is beautifully written and scathingly honest about its author's passionately mixed feelings towards OW and indeed himself.

Kael, Pauline, 'Raising Kane': see Mankiewicz, Herman J and Orson Welles, *Citizen Kane.*

Leaming, Barbara, *Orson Welles: A Biography* (Viking, New York: 1985): authorised, somewhat credulous biography featuring lengthy quotation from interviews with OW.

McBride, Joseph, *Orson Welles* (Secker & Warburg, London: 1972; revised and expanded edition, Da Capo Press, Massachusetts: 1996): perhaps the single most perceptive critical study of OW's films, this book earned its author a place in OW's inner circle and a role in the uncompleted *The Other Side of the Wind*.

Mac Liammóir, Micheál, *All for Hecuba* (Methuen, London: 1946): heady and poetic, these memoirs provide a wonderfully resonant portrait of the 16-year-old OW's arrival at Mac Liammóir's Gate Theatre in 1931 and their enduring (if not always harmonious) friendship.

Mac Liammóir, Micheál, *Put Money In Thy Purse* (Methuen, London: 1942): equally vivid and mellifluous account of the protracted production of OW's *Othello* – the author's first experience of film – taken from his journals.

Mankiewicz, Herman J, and Orson Welles, *Citizen Kane* (Secker & Warburg, New York: 1971): the shooting script, which differs subtly from the finished film and is prefaced with 'Raising *Kane*', the well-written but questionable *New Yorker* article in which critic Pauline Kael alleged that Mankiewicz deserved sole credit for writing the picture.

Mulvey, Laura, *Citizen Kane* (British Film Institute, London: 1992): a monograph by one of the UK's most respected and influential film academics, this is full of insight but its feminist and psychoanalytical critical apparatus can seem dry to non-initiates.

Naremore, James, *The Magic World of Orson Welles* (OUP, Oxford: 1978; revised edition, 1989): excellent critical study of OW's films.

Perkins, V F, *The Magnificent Ambersons* (British Film Institute, London: 1999): an engaging critique of the picture and account of its troubled production history.

Thomson, David, *Rosebud: The Story of Orson Welles* (Little Brown, St Ives: 1996): the most lively and readable biography to date, Thomson's novelistic approach is psychologically gripping but to be taken with a pinch of salt.

Tynan, Kenneth, *The Diaries of Kenneth Tynan*, edited by John Lahr (Bloomsbury, London: 2001): the diaries of a devotee, protégé and collaborator of OW who was later disillusioned by Pauline Kael's 'Raising *Kane*'.

Welles, Orson, *The Cradle Will Rock* (Santa Teresa Press, California: 1994): the unproduced screenplay for OW's own film of his scandalous 1937 Broadway production.

Welles, Orson, *Mr Arkadin* (Panther Books, St Albans: 1974): credited to OW, the novelisation of the film also known as *Confidential Report* was in fact probably written by his colleague Maurice Bessy.

Welles, Orson, and Peter Bogdanovich, *This Is Orson Welles*, edited by Jonathan Rosenbaum (HarperCollins, New York: 1992): this collection of interviews between OW and his younger friend and admirer – himself an acclaimed director – was decades in the making thanks to OW's procrastinations, lost material and editing difficulties. It offers a terrific store of OW's opinions on his own career and related subjects, along with useful endnotes and supplementary material. Rosenbaum's chronology remains the most meticulous available and the present book's chronology is indebted to it.

Welles, Orson, and Oja Kodar, *The Big Brass Ring* (Black Spring Press, California: 1987): OW's unproduced attempt at a commercial screenplay, which nonetheless remains entirely characteristic.

White, Rob, *The Third Man* (British Film Institute, London: 2003): incisive account of the unusual joint effort that resulted in *The Third Man*, with a chapter focusing on OW's charismatic contribution.

Picture Sources

The author and publishers wish to express their thanks to the following sources of illustrative material and/or permission to reproduce it. They will make proper acknowledgerments in future editions in the event that any omissions have occurred.

Corbis: pp. vi, 18 30, 50, 60, 78, 122, 136; Getty Images: pp. 3, 11, 31, 45, 63, 67, 71, 79, 93, 110, 144; Kitchen Sink Press Inc: pp. 141; Lebrecht Picture Library/Interfoto: p 49; Lebrecht Picture Library/Rue des Archives: pp. i, ii, 21, 85, 86, 90, 92, 105, 112, 116; 120, 134; Mary Evans Picture Library: p. 38; Ben Walters: p. 88; Workman Publishing: p 108.

Index

LIFE & TIMES FROM HAUS

Churchill
by Sebastian Haffner
'One of the most brilliant things of
any length ever written about
Churchill.' *TLS*
1-904341-07-1 (pb) £8.99
1-904341-06-3 (hb) £12.99

Dietrich
by Malene Skaerved
'It is probably the best book ever on
Marlene.' C. Downes
1-904341-13-6 (pb) £8.99
1-904341-12-8 (hb) £12.99

Beethoven
by Martin Geck
'. . . this little gem is a truly handy
reference.' *Musical Opinion*
1-904341-00-4 (pb) £8.99
1-904341-03-9 (hb) £12.99

Prokofiev
by Thomas Schipperges
'beautifully made, . . . well-produced
photographs, . . . with useful
historical nuggets.' *The Guardian*
1-904341-32-2 (pb) £8.99
1-904341-34-9 (hb) £12.99

Curie
by Sarah Dry
'. . . this book could hardly be bettered'
New Scientist
selected as **Outstanding Academic Title**
by *Choice*
1-904341-29-2 (pb) £8.99

Einstein
by Peter D Smith
'Concise, complete, well-produced and
lively throughout, . . . a bargain at the
price.' *New Scientist*
1-904341-15-2 (pb) £8.99
1-904341-14-4 (hb) £12.99

Casement
by Angus Mitchell
'hot topic' *The Irish Times*
1-904341-41-1 (pb) £8.99

Britten
by David Matthews
'I have read them all – but none with as
much enjoyment as this.' *Literary Review*
1-904341-21-7 (pb) £8.99
1-904341-39-X (hb) £12.99

De Gaulle
by Julian Jackson
'this concise and distinguished book'
Andrew Roberts *Sunday Telegraph*
1-904341-44-6 (pb) £8.99

Orwell
by Scott Lucas
'short but controversial assessment . . .
is sure to raise a few eyebrows' *Sunday
Tasmanian*
1-904341-33-0 (pb) £8.99

Bach
by Martin Geck
'The production values of the book are
exquisite, too.'
The Guardian
1-904341-16-0 (pb) £8.99
1-904341-35-7 (hb) £12.99

Kafka
by Klaus Wagenbach
'One of the most useful books about Kafka
ever published' *Frankfurter Allgemeine
Zeitung*
1-904341-02 -0 (PB) £8.99
1-904341-01-2 (hb) £12.99

Dostoevsky
by Richard Freeborn
'. . . wonderful . . . a learned guide'
The Sunday Times
1-904341-27-6 (pb) £8.99

Brahms
by Hans Neunzig
'readable, comprehensive and
attractively priced'
The Irish Times
1-904341-17-9 (pb) £8.99

Verdi
by Barbara Meier
'These handy volumes fill a gap in the
market . . . admirably.' *Classic fM*
1-904341-21-7 (pb) £8.99
1-904341-39-X (hb) L12.99

Armstrong
by David Bradbury
'generously illustrated . . . a fine and well-
researched introduction' George Melly
Daily Mail
1-904341-46-2 (pb) £8.99
1-904341-47-0 (hb) £12.99